HOW
TO
FIX
YOUR
CREDIT

OTHER BOOKS IN THE ESPERANZA SERIES

(also available in Spanish)

Now Available

How to Buy a Home

There Is an Answer: How to Prevent and Understand
   HIV/AIDS

Coming Soon

How to Write a Résumé and Get a Job

U.S. Citizenship for You and Your Family

ESPERANZA SERIES

HOW TO FIX YOUR CREDIT

THE REVEREND LUIS CORTÉS JR.

with Karin Price Mueller

ATRIA BOOKS

New York London Toronto Sydney

ATRIA BOOKS
1230 Avenue of the Americas
New York, NY 10020

Copyright © 2006 by Luis Cortés, Jr.

Library of Congress Cataloging-in-Publication Data
Cortés, Luis, Reverend.
    How to fix your credit / Luis Cortés Jr. with Karin Price Mueller.
    p. cm. — (Esperanza series)
Includes bibliographical references.
1. Consumer credit—United States. 2. Consumer credit—United States—Religious
aspects. 3. Finance, personal—United States. I. Mueller, Karin Price, 1970– II. Title.
HG3756.U54C689 2006
332.024'02—dc22   2006048973

ISBN-13: 978-0-7432-8791-3

First Atria Books trade paperback edition October 2006

10 9 8 7 6 5 4 3 2 1

Atria Books is a trademark of Simon & Schuster, Inc.

Manufactured in the United States of America

For information regarding special discounts for bulk purchases,
please contact Simon & Schuster Special Sales at
1-800-456-6798 or business@simonandschuster.com

CONTENTS

INTRODUCTION   ix

PREFACE   xi

STEP 1. HOW LENDERS SEE YOU   1

YOUR CREDIT REPORT   1

WHAT'S IN YOUR REPORT   2

GETTING A FREE COPY OF YOUR CREDIT REPORTS   2

WHAT YOUR CREDIT REPORT LOOKS LIKE   4

WHAT TO DO WITH YOUR REPORTS   4

IF YOU FIND A MISTAKE   5

YOUR CREDIT SCORE   15

GETTING YOUR FICO SCORE   16

NEW KIND OF CREDIT SCORE   17

IMPROVING YOUR CREDIT SCORE   18

BEWARE OF CREDIT REPAIR SERVICES   19

STEP 2. UNDERSTANDING DEBT   21

HOW MUCH DEBT DO YOU HAVE?   21

HOW MUCH DEBT IS TOO MUCH?   23

UNDERSTANDING HOW INTEREST RATES WORK   23

REVOLVING DEBT   24

INSTALLMENT DEBT   25

GOOD DEBT VERSUS BAD DEBT   26

STEP 3. STOP OVERSPENDING   28

LIVE ON A CASH ONLY BASIS   28

EVALUATE YOUR SPENDING HABITS   20

WANTS VERSUS NEEDS   30

SET A BUDGET   31

SHOP SMARTER   36

STEP 4. NEGOTIATE WITH YOUR CREDITORS   38

WHY BANKRUPTCY ISN'T AN OPTION   38

HOW BANKRUPTCY WORKS   39

CHAPTER 7   40

CHAPTER 13   41

LET'S MAKE A DEAL   42

RESPONDING TO DEBT COLLECTORS   45

IF YOU'RE FACING EVICTION   46

STEP 5. PAY ON TIME   48

SET YOURSELF UP FOR SUCCESS   48

ORGANIZE YOUR PAYMENTS   51

WHO'S HELPING WHOM?   52

USING CREDIT CARDS WISELY   53

SHOPPING FOR THE BEST DEALS ON CREDIT CARDS   54

STEP 6. PAY IT OFF   58

WHAT TO PAY FIRST?   58

CREDIT COUNSELING SERVICES AND
    DEBT CONSOLIDATION   61

SHOULD I TRANSFER MY CREDIT CARD BALANCES?   66

STEP 7. ADD POSITIVE INFORMATION TO YOUR FILE   68

MANAGE THE CREDIT YOU HAVE   68

APPLY FOR A SECURED CREDIT CARD   69

APPLY FOR A SMALL LOAN   71

THE COSIGNING OPTION   72

PATIENCE IS THE KEY   72

STEP 8. DON'T GET RIPPED OFF: PART 1   73

AUTO FINANCING   73

KNOW WHAT YOU CAN AFFORD   74

NEGOTIATING THE PRICE   74

EXPLORE YOUR FINANCING OPTIONS   77

IF YOU CAN'T PAY   79

A NEW SCAM EVERY DAY   80

MORTGAGES AND PREDATORY LENDING   80

TYPES OF MORTGAGES   81

COSTS AND FEES   83

SIGNS OF PREDATORY LENDING   84

GOVERNMENT PROGRAMS   85

STEP 9. DON'T GET RIPPED OFF: PART 2   87

PAYDAY LOANS   87

REFUND ANTICIPATION LOANS   89

COSIGNED DEBT   91

STEP 10. AVOID MAKING THE SAME MISTAKES AGAIN   93

MAINTAIN SELF-CONTROL   93

PAY YOURSELF FIRST: SAVINGS PLANS   95

EMERGENCY FUNDS   96

THE STOCK MARKET   98

LONG-TERM SAVINGS PLANS   99

OTHER TAX ADVANTAGES   103

   EARNED INCOME TAX CREDIT (EITC)   103

   CHILD AND DEPENDENT CARE CREDIT   104

   CHILD TAX CREDIT   105

EPILOGUE   106

ACKNOWLEDGMENTS   109

SOURCES   111

INTRODUCTION

Credit is a tool that allows us to enjoy something today with the money we will earn tomorrow. It also provides insight into who we are as spiritual beings. Sacred scripture shares many texts that refer to money or finance. Among them we find one of the most often quoted scriptures, "For the love of money is a source of all kinds of evil. Some have been so eager to have it that they have wandered away from the faith and have broken their hearts with many sorrows" (*Good News Bible*, American Bible Society, 1 Timothy 6:10).

This scripture explains how money can switch from being simply a tool to becoming the focus of one's life. We must understand that credit is available to us for the immediate purchase of a necessary and affordable item. As people of faith, it is important that we understand when it is appropriate to use credit. Too many of us borrow from the future to acquire things that we really don't need in the present. If you are thinking of borrowing from your future, you should ask yourself, Why am I borrowing from my future earnings? Am I borrowing from the future to invest in the present so that my future can be better? Can I save for this instead of using credit? For most of us the decisions we make are either/or decisions. We purchase one thing or another on credit, but too many of those purchases are not investments for the future but purchases that take up our future earnings, plus interest, to serve an unnecessary immediate desire. I am not advocating that we not have a new TV set or a new car, but that we use good judgment. Credit should be used first and foremost to help you, your family, and your community. If we can focus on what is most important—the development of our spiritual, academic, and intellectual lives—we are on the way to healthier economic status. So let's learn about credit, and if we need to, let's repair yours.

PREFACE

Trouble with credit is a problem you can't ignore. No matter how much money you earn or where you live, if you've made mistakes with credit in the past, those mistakes will haunt you—unless you empower yourself to fix your credit. And you can.

Say you have $5,000 in credit card debt, at 18 percent annual interest. If you make only the minimum payment each month, you'll be hanging on to that debt for a whopping 313 months, or more than 26 years. You'll pay more than $7,100 in interest costs—a far higher amount than your original debt.

Don't get scared off by the numbers. Any amount of debt, no matter how scary it sounds, can be paid, with a little planning and a lot of determination.

First, know you're not alone. About 51 million American households carry credit card debt, at an average balance of nearly $12,000, according to cardweb.com. And the reason is more than just overspending. We're not always paying on time, and we're not always being smart about the money we owe. Americans shelled out more than $24 billion in credit card fees last year, including late-payment fees and over-limit fees.

Before you can fix your problems, you need to understand why troubles with credit can be so damaging. If you don't have a good credit history, you'll struggle to get ahead financially. It may be hard to get a mortgage to buy a home, or a loan to buy a car. Or if lenders do decide to allow you to borrow money, they won't give you very good terms. You'll pay excessively high interest rates for the privilege of borrowing money. That's because if you haven't had a responsible payment history in the past, lenders aren't going to want to take you on as a risk.

But again, you can fix this. It takes patience, time, and dogged determination, but you can clean up your credit history and become attractive to lenders. This book will show you how.

HOW
TO
FIX
YOUR
CREDIT

STEP 1

HOW LENDERS SEE YOU

Lenders don't want to treat you like a number or a piece of paper. But lenders are running a business, and they have constraints. They have to work within certain rules, using a series of formulas, before lending you money. It doesn't matter if you're nice, if you've lost your job, or if a bad relationship has left you in a financial hole. Lenders have to depend on a series of written reports, and a number, to learn everything they need to know about you. What is most influential in making their decision is your credit history.

YOUR CREDIT REPORT

The written report that lenders depend on is called your credit report. A credit report is essentially a history of your entire financial life, from your first credit card to the present time.

There are three major companies that track your credit. They're called credit bureaus. These companies—Equifax, TransUnion, and Experian—all keep similar records of your credit history. When a lender is considering giving you a loan or a credit card, the lender will contact one of the three credit bureaus for a copy of your credit history. On the basis of the information in your file, the lender will decide whether or not to take a risk with you, how much to lend you, and at what interest rate.

WHAT'S IN YOUR REPORT

Each credit bureau uses a different format for the information it collects, but all three bureaus have basically the same information. You'll first find identifying information, such as your name, your Social Security number or Individual Taxpayer Identification Number (ITIN), and your address. Your employment information will also appear here.

Next, you'll find a listing of all the credit accounts you've ever had. This will show if the account is closed or current; when the account was opened (and closed, if it's been closed); your credit limit or loan amount; the account balance; and your payment history. This is where lenders will see if you've been paying your accounts on time.

Then comes a section on inquiries. An inquiry takes place when someone asks for a copy of your credit report. Inquiries may come from lenders, from landlords, or from employers. The report lists both voluntary inquiries, which are ones that come when you give lenders permission to check your report when you apply for credit; and involuntary inquiries, which come when lenders order your report on their own—for example, if they want to send you a preapproved credit offer in the mail.

Finally, your credit report will have a section that includes information of public record, usually based on papers filed in a court of law. This can include information on collection agencies seeking funds from you, bankruptcies, foreclosures, overdue alimony or child support payments, lawsuits, liens, wage attachments, and judgments. It may also include arrest records.

GETTING A FREE COPY
OF YOUR CREDIT REPORTS

If your credit history shows you've made late payments in the past, or if you've taken out loans you've never repaid, you may have a hard time getting a new lender to lend you any money. And if lenders are willing to lend you money, they're going to charge a very high interest rate—to the point that you may be paying more in interest than you borrowed in the first place.

That's why it's so important to have a good credit history. If you want to buy a car, get a mortgage, get a credit card, or rent an apartment, the people you want to do business with will want to know you're a good risk. Having a good credit report will save you money and allow you to accomplish many of your financial goals.

It's very possible that your credit report has some errors. It may show that you're delinquent on an account, when in reality that account should be clean. This is why it's essential for you to get a copy of your credit report, read it, understand it, and make sure it's accurate.

New legislation passed in Congress—the Fair and Accurate Credit Transactions Act (FACT Act)—allows everyone to get free copies of his or her credit reports from the three major credit bureaus once a year. To get your free reports, you must call 877-322-8228, or visit www.AnnualCreditReport.com. This is a centralized service created by the three credit bureaus to help consumers access their reports in one place (while helping the bureaus keep track of which consumers have ordered their reports).

Warning: If you go to the Web site, make sure to spell the Web address very carefully. There are imposter sites that have similar spellings, and if you end up at these sites by mistake, they're going to tell you about other services, which you need to pay for before you get your reports. It's a scam to try to get you to pay for services you don't necessarily need. The AnnualCreditReport.com site is perfectly safe. But the Federal Trade Commission (FTC)—the government agency that deals with consumer protection and other economic issues touching the lives of most Americans—warns that consumers must be careful not to be fooled by these other sites. The FTC recently settled a lawsuit against a company that promised "free" reports, but these weren't really free. If you're nervous about making a mistake when you type a Web address, you can go to the FTC Web site at www.ftc.gov. There, you'll find a link to the authentic AnnualCreditReport.com site. Or simply visit the Esperanza USA site (www.esperanza.us) for a direct link.

You can also contact the three credit bureaus directly for copies of your reports, but the copies are free only if you go through the site mentioned above. The three credit reporting agencies—Equifax, Experian, and Trans-Union—offer essentially the same information in their credit reports. Only the layout is slightly different. If you order through AnnualCreditReport.com, you can get all three for free. You want to make sure they're all accurate, because while no one report is more important than the others, you don't know which one your lender will see.

WHAT YOUR CREDIT REPORT LOOKS LIKE

On pages 6–12 you will see an example of what you can find on Experian's report.

WHAT TO DO WITH YOUR REPORTS

Read, read, read. Carefully go through each entire report and make sure there are no errors. Errors are common. According to a study done in 2004 by the U.S. Public Interest Research Group (U.S. PIRG), as many as

79 percent of credit reports have errors. According to the study, 25 percent of those errors were serious enough that credit could easily have been denied to consumers because of the wrong information. The study is called "Mistakes Do Happen: A Look at Errors in Consumer Credit Reports."

The Web sites of the three credit bureaus have very explicit directions on how to read their reports, which all look somewhat different. Read the directions to understand how each bureau presents the information. If you see something you don't understand, call the bureau's toll-free number. A customer service representative can help you translate the jargon, or explain anything else that doesn't make sense to you.

IF YOU FIND A MISTAKE

To fix mistakes on your reports, you have to take charge. This process is called "dispute."

If you want to dispute an item on your report, the first step is to contact the credit bureau by writing a letter, explaining the error you've found. The credit bureau will open an investigation, which will probably include contacting the lender who told the bureau that, for example, you missed a few payments. The lender will then review the information and report back to the bureau with its findings. If the credit bureau agrees that the item on your report is an error, the bureau will make the change in your report. By law, the companies have 30 days to investigate and report back to you on their findings.

If you need help writing a dispute letter, the Federal Trade Commission offers a sample letter, available on page 13.

experian°

Online Personal Credit Report from Experian for

Experian credit report prepared for
JOHN Q CONSUMER
Your report number is
1562064065
Report date
01/24/2005

1

Index:
- Potentially negative items
- Accounts in good standing
- Requests for your credit history
- Personal information
- Important message from Experian
- Contact us

2

Experian collects and organizes information about you and your credit history from public records, your creditors and other reliable sources. Experian makes your credit history available to your current and prospective creditors, employers and others as allowed by law, which can expedite your ability to obtain credit and can make offers of credit available to you. We do not grant or deny credit; each credit grantor makes that decision based on its own guidelines.

Potentially Negative Items

back to top

Public Records

3

Credit grantors may carefully review the items listed below when they check your credit history. Please note that the account information connected with some public records, such as bankruptcy, also may appear with your credit items listed later in this report.

MAIN COUNTY CLERK

Address: Identification Number: Plaintiff:
123 MAINTOWN S   1   ANY COMMISSIONER O.
BUFFALO , NY 10000

Status: Status Details:
Civil claim paid.   This item was verified and updated on 06-2001.

Date Filed: Claim Amount:
10/15/2000 $200
Date Resolved: Liability
01/04/2001   Amount:
                 NA

Report number:
You will need your report number to contact Experian online, by phone or by mail.

Index:
Navigate through the sections of your credit report using these links.

Potentially negative items:
Items that creditors may view less favorably. It includes the creditor's name and address, your account number (shortened for security), account status, type and terms of the account and any other information reported to Experian by the creditor. Also includes any bankruptcy, lien and judgment information obtained directly from the courts.

7

Responsibility:
INDIVIDUAL

Credit Items

For your protection, the last few digits of your account numbers do not display.

ABCD BANKS

Address: Account Number:
100 CENTER RD   1000000....
BUFFALO, NY 10000
(555) 555-5555
Status: Paid/Past due 60 days.

4

Date Opened:	Type:	Credit Limit/Original Amount:
10/1997	Installment	$523
Reported Since:	Terms:	High Balance:
11/1997	12 Months	NA
Date of Status:	Payment:	Recent Balance:
01/1999	Monthly	$0 as of 01/1999
	Payment:	Recent Payment:
	$0	$0
Last Reported:	Responsibility:	
01/1999	Individual	

Account History:
60 days as of 12-1998
30 days as of 11-1998

Status:

Indicates the current status of the account.

If you believe information in your report is inaccurate, you can dispute that item quickly, effectively and cost free by using Experian's online dispute service located at:

www.experian.com/disputes

Disputing online is the fastest way to address any concern you may have about the information in your credit report.

8

MAIN COLL AGENCIES

Address: Account Number: Original Creditor:
PO BOX 123   0123456789   TELEVISE CABLE COMM.
ANYTOWN, PA 10000
(555) 555-5555

Status: Collection account. $95 past due as of 4-2000.

		Credit Limit/Original Amount:
Date Opened:	Type:	$95
01/2000	Installment	High Balance:
Reported Since:	Terms:	NA
04/2000	NA	Recent Balance:
Date of Status:	Monthly	$95 as of 04/2000
04/2000	Payment:	Recent Payment:
	$0	$0
Last Reported:	Responsibility:	
04/2000	Individual	

Your statement: ITEM DISPUTED BY CONSUMER

Account History:
Collection as of 4-2000

Accounts in Good Standing

back to top

AUTOMOBILE AUTO FINANCE

Address: Account Number:
100 MAIN ST E   12345678998....
SMALLTOWN, MD 90001
(555) 555-5555

Status: Open/Never late.

Accounts in good standing:

Lists accounts that have a positive status and may be viewed favorably by creditors. Some creditors do not report to us, so some of your accounts may not be listed.

Type:

Account type indicates whether your account is a revolving or an installment account.

Date Opened:	Type: **G**	Credit Limit/Original Amount:
01/2000	**Installment**	**$10,355**
Reported Since:	Terms:	High Balance:
01/2000	**65 Months**	NA
Date of Status:	**Monthly**	Recent Balance:
08/2001	Payment:	**$7,984 as of 08/2001**
	$210	Recent Payment:
Last Reported:	Responsibility:	$0
08/2001	**Individual**	

MAIN

Address: Account Number:
PO BOX 1234   1234567899876
FORT LAUDERDALE, FL 10009
Status: Closed/Never late.

Date Opened:	Type:	Credit Limit/Original Amount:
03/1991	**Revolving**	NA
Reported Since:	Terms:	High Balance:
03/1991	**1 Months**	**$3,228**
Date of Status:	**Monthly**	Recent Balance:
08/2000	Payment:	**$0 /paid as of 08/2000**
	$0	Recent Payment:
Last Reported:	Responsibility:	$0
08/2000	**Individual**	

Your statement:
Account closed at consumer's request

Requests for Your Credit History   **7**

back to top

Requests Viewed By Others

We make your credit history available to your current and prospective creditors and employers as allowed by law. Personal data about you may be made available to companies whose products and services may interest you.

The section below lists all who have requested in the recent past to review your credit history as a result of actions involving you, such as the completion of a credit application or the transfer of an account to a collection agency, mortgage or loan application, etc. Creditors may view these requests when evaluating your creditworthiness.

HOMESALE REALTY CO

Address:
2000 S MAINROAD BLVD STE
ANYTOWN CA 11111
(555) 555-5555

Date of Request:
07/16/2001

Comments:
Real estate loan on behalf of 1000 COPRORATE COMPANY. This inquiry is scheduled to continue on record until 8-2003.

ABC BANK

Address:
PO BOX 100
BUFFALO NY 10000
(555) 555-5555

Date of Request:
02/23/2001

Comments:
Permissible purpose. This inquiry is scheduled to continue on record until 3-2003.

ANYTOWN FUNDING INC

Address:
100 W MAIN AVE STE 100
INTOWN CA 10000
(555) 555-5555

Date of Request:
07/25/2000

Comments:
Permissible purpose. This inquiry is scheduled to continue on record until 8-2002.

Requests for your credit history:

Also called "inquiries", requests for your credit history are logged on your report whenever anyone reviews your credit information. There are two types of inquiries.

Requests viewed by others

Inquiries resulting from a transaction initiated by you. These include inquiries from your applications for credit, housing or other loans. They also include transfer of an account to a collection agency. Creditors may view these items when evaluating your creditworthiness.

Requests viewed only by you

11

Requests Viewed Only By You

The section below lists all who have a permissible purpose by law and have requested in the recent past to review your information. You may not have initiated these requests, so you may not recognize each source. We offer information about you to those with a permissible purpose, for example, to:

* other creditors who want to offer you preapproved credit;
* an employer who wishes to extend an offer of employment;
* a potential investor in assessing the risk of a current obligation;
* Experian or other credit reporting agencies to process a report for you;
* your existing creditors to monitor your credit activity (date listed may reflect only the most recent request)

We report these requests only to you as a record of activities. We do not provide this information to other creditors who evaluate your creditworthiness.

MAIN BANK USA
Address:
1 MAIN CTR AA 11
BUFFALO NY 10000

Date of Request:
08/10/2001

MAINTOWN BANK
Address:
PO BOX 100
MAINTOWNS DE 10000
(555) 555-5555

Date of Request:
08/05/2001

ANYTOWN DATA CORPS
Address:
2000 S MAINTOWN BLVD STE
INTOWN CO 11111
(555) 555-5555

Date of Request:
07/16/2001

Inquiries resulting from transactions you may not have initiated but that are allowed under the FCRA. These include preapproved offers, as well as for employment, investment review, account monitoring by existing creditors, and requests by you for your own report. These items are shown only to you and have no impact on your creditworthiness or risk scores.

Personal Information **8**

The following information is reported to us by you, your creditors and other sources. Each source may report your personal information differently, which may result in variations of your name, address, Social Security number, etc. As part of our fraud-prevention program, a notice with additional information may appear. As a security precaution, the Social Security number that you used to obtain this report is not displayed. The Geographical Code shown with each address identifies the state, county, census tract, block group and Metropolitan Statistical Area associated with each address.

Names:
JOHN Q CONSUMER
JONATHON Q CONSUMER
J Q CONSUMER

Social Security number variations:
999999999

Year of birth:
1954

Employers:
ABCDE ENGINEERING CORP

Telephone numbers:
(555) 555 5555 Residential

Address: 123 MAIN STREET
ANYTOWN, MD 90001-9999
Type of Residence: Multifamily
Geographical Code: 0-156510-31-8840

Address: 555 SIMPLE PLACE
ANYTOWN, MD 90002-7777
Type of Residence: Single family
Geographical Code: 0-176510-33-8840

Address: 999 HIGH DRIVE APT 15B
ANYTOWN, MD 90003-5555
Type of Residence: Apartment complex
Geographical Code: 0-156510-31-8840

9

Your Personal Statement **10**

No general personal statements appear on your report.

Important Message From Experian

back to top

By law, we cannot disclose certain medical information (relating to physical, mental, or behavioral health or condition). Although we do not generally collect such information, it could appear in the name of a data furnisher (i.e., "Cancer Center") that reports your payment history to us. If so, those names display in your report, but in reports to others they display only as MEDICAL PAYMENT DATA. Consumer statements included on your report at your request that contain medical information are disclosed to others.

Personal information:

Personal information associated with your history that has been reported to Experian by you, your creditors and other sources.

May include name and Social Security number variations, employers, telephone numbers, etc. Experian lists all variations so you know what is being reported to us as belonging to you.

Address information:

Your current address and previous address(es)

Personal statement:

Any personal statement that you added to your report appears here.

Note - statements remain as part of the report for 2 years and display to anyone who has permission to review your report.

Date
Your Name
Your Address
Your City, State, Zip Code

Complaint Department
Name of Company
Address
City, State, Zip Code

Dear Sir or Madam:

I am writing to dispute the following information in my file. I have circled the items I dispute on the attached copy of the report I received.

This item (identify item(s) disputed by name of source, such as creditors or tax court, and identify type of item, such as credit account, judgment, etc.) is (inaccurate or incomplete) because (describe what is inaccurate or incomplete and why). I am requesting that the item be removed (or request another specific change) to correct the information.

Enclosed are copies of (use this sentence if applicable and describe any enclosed documentation, such as payment records, court documents) supporting my position. Please reinvestigate this (these) matter(s) and (delete or correct) the disputed item(s) as soon as possible.

Sincerely,
Your name

Enclosures: (list what you are enclosing)

You can also visit www.esperanza.us for more sample letters.

If one credit bureau has a mistake in your file, there's a good chance that the same mistake will appear on your other reports, too. Compare your two other credit reports to make sure they don't have the same mistake. If they do, notify those bureaus of the errors. Also, be aware that the lender who misreported the information to the first bureau is required to make the correction at all three bureaus. Still, it's smart to make sure that this happens.

If the investigation into your complaint goes your way, great. The lender is then required to give you the results in writing, and if the investigation leads to a change to your report, the bureau must give you another free report. (This doesn't count as one of your annual free reports.) If the mistake has been fixed, you can request that the bureau contact all those who received the inaccurate report in the past six months (or the past two years, for employers) to tell them of the correction.

If the investigation doesn't turn out as you hoped, and the credit bureau and the lender insist that the information is accurate, there's not much you can do to change it. But what you can do is add a short written statement to your credit file to explain your side of the story. You can do this free. Your written statement will then become part of your credit report, and anyone who wants to see your report will also see your version of events. Here's a sample letter.

Date
Your Name
Your Address
Your City, State, Zip Code

Name of Credit Bureau
Credit Bureau Address
City, State, Zip Code

Dear Sir or Madam:
I disagree with (identify the item you are disputing here). I took the following action: (explain the action you

took to pay the item here, and include dates if you have them). I have disputed the item but the company says (explain what the company's side is here). I have included here copies of (list here any proof you have of your actions).

Sincerely,
Your name

It's important to understand that you can't dispute negative information that's true and accurate. The only way true bad marks on your credit report, such as a bankruptcy, will vanish, is after the passage of time.

YOUR CREDIT SCORE

Your credit score is the next big item you'll need to tackle if you're trying to improve your credit. A credit score is simply a computer-generated number based on the information in your credit reports. Lenders use this number to determine whether or not you'll be a good credit risk. They use this number to decide whether to lend you money, and if so, how much to lend and at what interest rate.

The most influential credit score is called the FICO score. It's created by a company called Fair Isaac Corporation, and it's the credit score used by the three major credit bureaus. You have a separate FICO score with each of the three bureaus, because your credit file may be different at each bureau.

FICO scores range from 300 to 850. The higher your number, the better. The average FICO score is 723. If yours is lower, you need to take steps to improve your credit report; doing so will improve your FICO score.

FICO scores are calculated on the basis of several factors.

Your payment history has the biggest impact on your

score (35 percent). This includes late payments, missed payments, and negative public records, such as bankruptcies and wage attachments, or how well you've met your past obligations.

The next most important factor (30 percent) is how much you owe. Lenders like to see that you've been successful with both revolving credit (credit cards) and installment loans (car loans and mortgages). They also want to see if you've maxed out all your available credit.

FICO scores also take into account the length of your credit history (15 percent). The longer you've been using credit and paying your obligations, the better, as this shows lenders that you're more likely to pay in the future. The score also includes information on new credit (10 percent), and how many recent inquiries you've had. And finally, the score includes details on the types of credit you use (10 percent).

Your FICO score does not consider personal information on your credit report, such as your race, religion, national origin, age, or gender, or where you live.

GETTING YOUR FICO SCORE

Unlike your credit report, your FICO score isn't available free. There are several ways to get your FICO score. At the FICO Web site, www.myfico.com, you can order your three FICO scores (the ones used by the three major credit bureaus) for $14.95. Or you can call 800-319-4433.

You can also get your FICO score through the credit bureaus, but this will also involve paying a fee. Depending on what you order, it may cost between $5 and $35 for your scores (which are usually sold with copies of your credit reports).

If you've applied for credit, the lender will probably have obtained your FICO score from one of the bureaus.

You can ask the lender to tell you the score (this wouldn't cost you anything), but only mortgage lenders are required by law to disclose your score. A credit card company or another lender may or may not share the information with you. But, before you pay for your score, it never hurts to ask.

NEW KIND OF CREDIT SCORE

The three credit bureaus have announced the creation of a new kind of credit score, which they say will simplify the process. The bureaus say there are two variables in calculating a credit score: the data (your credit history as reported by each bureau) and the scoring methodology (the math used to calculate your score). In what the bureaus say is an attempt to make credit scoring easier to understand and more consistent, they've created a new credit score, called VantageScore. To calculate the score, which can range from 501 to 990 (the higher the score, the better), the bureaus each use the same methodology. For example, each bureau collects credit information independently, so it is possible that the exact same information may not be on all three files. With other credit scores, the bureaus say even if the same information is in your files, your credit score could be different because of the different calculations used. They say with Vantage-Score, if the same information were on each file, the scores would be identical—all because they'll use the same calculations to get your score.

The bureaus say consumers who have a short credit history often end up with low scores under other credit-scoring models. They say VantageScore will give "more predictive scores" on consumers with limited credit histories, which would reduce the need for creditors to go through a manual review process and impose their own personal methodology to determine credit worthiness.

Because VantageScore is so new, at the time of this book's printing the pricing for these scores, which will be sold separately by each credit bureau, was not available. The average VantageScore was not yet available either. But if lenders start using these new credit scores as they currently use FICO scores, you should be able to find the prices at each of the three credit bureaus both online and via telephone.

IMPROVING YOUR CREDIT SCORE

If your FICO score is less than 723, or if your VantageScore is less than what the bureaus say is the average score, you'll want to make some improvements. Unfortunately, nothing happens overnight. Improving your score will take a lot of discipline, and time.

The most important thing you can do to improve your score is to be vigilant about your current debts, no matter how much you owe.

You must start making all your payments on time, even if you're able to pay only the minimum due. On-time payments will show lenders you're being responsible about the money you owe, and that makes you a better credit risk. Next, you need to work toward paying off your debt. Not only will you show lenders that you can pay your bills; you'll show that you're not simply borrowing and borrowing more, without the ability to pay.

There's no magic number of months or years it will take to improve your score. Each month of positive information will work in your favor. Remember to have patience and to keep your long-term goal—having good credit—in mind. (Read Steps 5, 6, and 7 for more detailed strategies on how to pay on time, how to reduce or eliminate your debt, and how to add more positive information to your credit reports.)

BEWARE OF CREDIT REPAIR SERVICES

Having a low FICO score and negative information on your credit reports might tempt you to find a quick fix. That's where credit repair services come in, preying on people with bad credit. For a fee of hundreds or even thousands of dollars, they promise the world: "Credit problems? No problem!" "We guarantee to make your bad credit vanish!" "We can wipe clean bankruptcies and bad loans from your credit report!"

It's all a lie, according to the FTC. Credit repair services pledge to do the impossible, and they often use illegal strategies to try to clean up your credit. They take a lot of money from you, and you may get nothing in return. Don't go to them. The only things that will improve your credit are time and positive, responsible financial moves on your part.

The FTC says you should watch for these warning signs about credit repair companies:

• Companies that want you to pay for credit repair services before they provide any services.

• Companies that do not tell you your legal rights and what you can do, free, for yourself.

• Companies that tell you not to contact a credit reporting company directly.

• Companies that suggest that you try to invent a "new" credit identity—and then get a new credit report—by applying for an Employer Identification Number to use instead of your Social Security number.

• Companies that advise you to dispute all information in your credit report or take any action that seems illegal, like creating a new credit identity.

You could end up in jail. Even though a company may be advising you, it's your responsibility to stay within the law. It's a federal crime to lie on a loan or credit application, and you could be charged with mail fraud or wire fraud if you use the mail or telephone to apply for credit under false pretenses.

Companies that make these promises can't legally remove negative information from your report. The only things these companies can do for you are things you can already do for yourself, free (such as disputing an error on your report).

By law, before you sign a contract with a credit repair company, it must give you a copy of a document called "Consumer Credit File Rights Under State and Federal Law." It describes what repair companies can and can't do by law. For example, they can't make false claims about the services they can perform for you, and they can't charge you until they've completed the services they've promised you. They must also give you a three-day waiting period, during which you can change your mind and back out of any contract you've signed with them.

They must give you a written contract that will give you a detailed description of the services they can provide and exactly what these services will cost you. They must also tell you how long it will take for them to get results.

If you've used a credit repair company already, and it hasn't delivered what it promised, or if you suspect that it's done something illegal, you should report the company to the office of your state's attorney general. Check the phone book for your local number, or go online to www.naag.org for a list of state attorneys general.

STEP 2

UNDERSTANDING DEBT

Like most Americans, you've probably accumulated a considerable amount of debt. You probably have a general idea about how much you owe, but you probably haven't added it all together lately. It's disheartening to see the total in black and white, especially if your credit report includes some negative marks. But you can take control of your financial situation. Doing so starts with honesty.

If you were trying to lose weight, you'd step on the scale to see where you are today, so you'd know how many pounds you want to lose. No matter how ugly the truth may be, you have to look it square in the face.

Now is the time to be honest with yourself about exactly how much you owe. Unless you truly understand how much debt you have, you can't come up with a plan to eliminate it—at least, not a plan that's going to work.

You're going to examine your personal debt and figure out how it works—how the interest is calculated, which debt you should try to pay off first, and which debt it might be smart to hold on to.

HOW MUCH DEBT DO YOU HAVE?

Don't guess. Collect the most recent statements from every kind of debt you have. If you know you've been charging a lot on your credit cards, call the 800 numbers on your statements for the most accurate and up-to-date amounts you owe.

Now get a piece of paper and get organized. Create a chart, and fill in the amounts you owe and the interest rates. Use a pencil, so you can erase old information and update the chart as you make payments. Here's a sample.

Lender	Amount Owed	Interest Rate	Next Payment	Due Date
Credit Card 1	$5,674	18.9%	$113 (minimum)	10/4
Credit Card 2	$3,954	23.0%	$79 (minimum)	10/7
Car Loan	$17,542	9.9%	$352.46	10/9
Doctor's Bill	$742	0%	$742	Past due

Now, find a place to post your chart. Choose the refrigerator, the bathroom mirror, or some other place where you'll see it often. I know—you probably don't want to look at it several times a day, but it's time to stop hiding from the reality of your debt. Instead of making you feel depressed, this chart should give you a boost. Each time you make a payment, you're going to update the chart, and you'll see your total debt shrinking. The chart will become something to smile about.

Not convinced? You're not a child, so you don't need gold stars as an incentive to do well. But you can give yourself something to look forward to once your debt is paid off. Do you have a goal such as taking a vacation, buying a new car, or buying something else that's special? Cut out a photo of what you want and keep it next to your chart. It will serve to remind you of why it's important to keep paying that debt.

HOW MUCH DEBT IS TOO MUCH?

Almost everyone carries some kind of debt, whether it's a mortgage, a car loan, a college loan, or credit cards. Most people need to borrow because we can't pay cash for jumbo purchases. But as you know, there can be too much debt in your life. It doesn't matter how much debt your neighbors, your friends, or your relatives have. What matters is how much you have, and whether or not you're able to meet your obligations.

How much is too much? There is no specific number. But if you're barely able to meet the minimum payments on your credit card, you have too much debt. If you're missing payments and defaulting on loans, you have too much debt. And if you're unable to save any money for long-term goals, you have too much debt.

Many financial professionals use a simple formula, called a debt ratio, to see if you have too much debt. They like to see a ratio of assets to debt no smaller than 2:1. That is, that you should have twice as much liquid assets as you have debt. For example, for every $1,000 of credit card debt you have, you should have $2,000 of cash in the bank.

UNDERSTANDING HOW INTEREST RATES WORK

Depending on the kind of debt you have, the interest rate may be calculated differently. And unfortunately, lots of credit cards, for example, have provisions that allow the lender to raise your interest rate if your payment is late.

Here are some terms you need to know and understand with regard to interest rates.

• *APR.* This stands for annual percentage rate. It is the same thing as the interest rate charged when you borrow.

• *Prime rate:* This is the rate the nation's largest banks will give their best customers for loans. Lenders use the prime rate as a base for setting the interest rates they charge the general public for credit cards and other loans. Your interest rate might be "prime plus 9 percent." (For example, in January 2005, the prime rate was 7.25 percent. A card that's prime plus 9 percent would have an interest rate of 16.25 percent.) Most lenders use the prime rate as calculated by *The Wall Street Journal.* This rate can stay the same for years, or it can change several times a year.

• *Fixed rate or fixed APR:* This is an interest rate that will generally not change.

• *Variable rate or variable APR:* This rate will change. It's calculated on the basis of certain economic indicators, including the prime rate. When the indicators go up or down, so does the interest rate you pay.

• *Penalty rate:* If you're late on payments, your lender may be able to raise your rate to a predetermined penalty, as written in the fine print of your contract. Even if you have a perfect payment record with one lender, a clause in your contract called "universal default" may allow your credit card company to raise your interest rate because you were late with *another* lender. Lenders may even be able to raise your rate if they determine that you have too much debt on other cards or if you default on a loan.

Revolving Debt

Credit cards are called revolving debt. You'll have an overall limit to how much you can borrow, and each time you make payments, your credit limit "revolves" back to that limit. This is debt that doesn't have a set monthly payment. The minimum payment due each month will change, depending on how much you're using the credit. The amount of the minimum payment varies from credit card to credit card. Generally, it's somewhere between 2 and 4 percent of your balance. So if you owe $2,000 and the minimum payment is 2 percent of your balance, the payment that month is $40.

Most credit card interest charges are based on what's called your average daily balance. Your balances on all the days of the month are added together and then divided by the number of days in the month.

Some credit cards allow you to make different transactions, such as cash advances. For these, your interest rate is probably different from—and higher than—the rate for regular purchases.

When you make a payment on a revolving credit line—your credit card—part of the payment goes toward the interest charges, and part goes toward paying the actual balance you owe. Take that $40 minimum payment. Say the interest rate on this card is 15 percent. Divide the interest rate by 12 months, then multiply the number by your balance: $(0.15/12)$ x 2,000. In this case, $25 will go toward the interest costs and $15 will go toward paying off your debt. (If you have more than one interest rate on the card, usually your payment goes toward the part of your balance that's charged the lower interest rate.)

That's why it can take so long to pay down a credit card balance if you're making only minimum payments. The $2,000 balance on a card with 15 percent interest will take 264 months, or more than 22 years, to pay off. For the $2,000 you borrowed, you'll pay more than $2,780 in interest charges—more than the amount you borrowed.

You have to make more than the minimum payments on revolving debt if you ever want to have a clean slate.

Installment Debt

Installment debt is the kind of loan you'll have when

you take on a mortgage or buy a new car. You can also take installment loans from your bank; these are generally called personal loans.

When you take an installment loan, you're borrowing a fixed amount of money for a certain period of time. You'll make monthly payments that don't change from month to month (unless you take an installment loan that offers a variable interest rate—more on that when we talk about mortgages in Step 8).

When you start making payments on installment loans, at first your payments are mostly interest. As the life of the loan goes on, more of your payment will start going toward the amount you borrowed—the principal—and less will go toward the interest.

In general, you'll find that installment loans have a much better interest rate than revolving credit. Another advantage of these loans is that because they have a fixed payment plan, you'll know how much you need to pay each month. This knowledge should help your budget.

GOOD DEBT VERSUS BAD DEBT

You might feel that no debt is good, but this isn't true. There are times when taking on debt makes sense—for purchases that are almost impossible to pay for in a big chunk, such as buying a home—as long as you have a plan to pay it off.

Mortgages are one kind of good debt. Sure, you're borrowing a lot of money to buy a home, but you're getting a long-term investment in return. Most homes will gain value over time, so that when the mortgage payments are done, your home will—you hope—be worth more than what you paid for it. Also, buying a home is more than a financial decision. It's a change in lifestyle. Becoming a home owner—and obtaining a mortgage to do it—will give you a terrific sense of accomplishment for you and your family. (You can get more information on the process of buying a home in my book *How to Buy a Home*.)

Student loans are another kind of good debt. Education is an investment in yourself or your child. A college degree means that you'll earn more over your lifetime—as much as 73 percent more than those with only a high school diploma, according to the College Board.

Bad debt, by contrast, is just about every other kind of borrowing. It includes those items you're using a credit card to pay for. Very likely, they are items you can live without; and if you're not paying cash, these are probably items you don't need.

Bad debt in the form of credit cards will usually have a very high interest rate. And as I've already stated, it can take years to pay off, especially if you can't afford more than the minimum payment.

In general, it makes financial sense to keep your good debt, slowly paying it every month, because of the favorable interest rate and fixed monthly payment. But you should get rid of bad debt as soon as possible, paying off the credit cards with the highest interest rates first.

In Step 3, we'll talk about ways to eliminate your habit of building bad debt—by slowing down or stopping unnecessary spending, setting financial priorities, and learning how to live within your means.

STEP 3

STOP OVERSPENDING

No one said getting out of debt would be easy. In order to accomplish your goal of improving your life by repairing your credit and getting out of debt, you have to make some sacrifices today. This is a time for discipline and self-control. Forget about that name-brand shirt, that CD, that pair of designer sneakers, that new car. Of course such things are nice to have, but buying them is how you got into this mess. While you're digging yourself out, it's essential that you don't add to your debt by buying items you can't afford.

If you see something you want and the monthly bills are paid, okay, go ahead. We can't live like cloistered clergy, and we shouldn't. When we work hard, we should enjoy at least some of what we earn once in a while. But you have already spent months, perhaps years, overdoing it, enjoying a little too much, buying on credit because you "had to have" something. And now, with a mound of debt, you're regretting it.

So if you have to have something, once in a while, make it part of your budget. And pay cash.

LIVE ON A CASH-ONLY BASIS

While you are working to eliminate your debt, cash is king. Even if you think you have the self-control to stop spending on credit, keeping credit cards in your wallet is unwise. You need to remove the temptation.

Until your debt is gone, put your credit cards on ice. That's right, on ice. Take a cup of water and dump your credit cards inside. Then place the cup in the freezer. And leave it there.

The credit cards will still be there in case of a dire emergency. But other than losing the roof over your head, being unable to work or get to work, or being unable to get medical care, there probably won't be any real emergencies.

If you just like the feel of plastic instead of cash, consider a debit card. If you have a checking account at a bank, you probably have a debit card already. A debit card looks like a credit card, but instead letting you buy on credit, a debit card "debits" your checking account each time you use it. The money comes straight out of your bank account, and you're not borrowing. You're spending the cash you have on hand.

If you don't have a debit card, get one. If you aren't using your existing debit card, start. It's the same as paying cash—as long as you exercise some self-control. But be careful: most debit cards these days are linked to a credit card. If you overspend the balance in your checking account, you'll start buying on credit. Or, when you go to use the card, the cashier may ask, "Debit or credit?" If you choose credit, you'll be heading back down the debt trail.

EVALUATE YOUR SPENDING HABITS

You now need to take a very close look at where your money is going. Rent, food, and gasoline for your car may be obvious. But you're also spending money at plenty of places where you don't need to be spending it. Take a look at a simple morning cup of coffee. Let's say you buy a $1 cup of coffee each workday, five days a week, for 50 weeks. (Let's assume that during the other two weeks you're on vacation.) You're spending $250 a year on coffee. If you smoke a pack of cigarettes a day, at a cost of $5.50 a pack, you're spending $2,007 a year. If you buy lunch at McDonald's three days a week at $6 a pop, you're spending $936 a year on greasy burgers and fries.

No one's saying you shouldn't drink coffee, or smoke, or eat fast food. Just realize what those guilty pleasures are costing you. Could the money you're spending serve you better somewhere else? You'll decide as you start to track and analyze your spending.

WANTS VERSUS NEEDS

Most people use the word "need" without considering what it really means. Often, what they really mean is "want."

"I need a new dress."
"I need a piece of chocolate."
"I need a vacation."

It may feel as if you need those items, but they're really things you want. A "need" is something you can't live without, such as food, shelter, and medical care. A "want" is more or less everything else. You can live without your "wants." You may not always be happy without them. But you won't come to physical harm (or even mental harm) if you don't fulfill your "wants."

In today's world, it can be very hard to distinguish between needs and wants. Turn on the television or open a magazine, and you'll see hundreds of things you think you need—but do you need them? Do you really need brand-name sneakers? Cable television? Even a car?

When so many people in our lives spend so much

money on luxury items, it's easy to feel as if we, too, need these things. They make life convenient, they're fashionable, and so on, but they're essentially wants, not needs. There are even some things we can't imagine living without, such as electricity, that are really not needs.

Come on, you're saying, what's the big deal if I buy a new pair of sneakers or a candy bar now and then? When you're talking about one item, of course it doesn't seem like a big deal. But when you can't meet your debt obligations because you've spent too much money on things you don't really need, you have a problem. If you're behind in paying your bills, and if you're not saving any money, you need to learn to balance your wants and your needs.

It's time for another list. Make a list of all the things you spend money on. Label each item "need" or "want." Be honest with yourself. Keep this list handy. It will help you when you organize your budget.

If you can easily pay for your needs and have money left over, and if you're debt-free, you can start spending on your wants. But if one of your needs is to be debt-free, you shouldn't be spending much—or anything—on your wants.

SET A BUDGET

To many people, "budget" is an ugly word. It gives a feeling of sacrifice, restriction, limits, and relinquishing control. If you have a problem with the word "budget," use some other term instead, such as "spending plan" or "cash flow plan." But for our discussion here, it will be called a budget.

A budget is really the opposite of restriction or giving up control. You're taking control of your money. You're setting the priorities and deciding where you want to spend your money, instead of just letting money dribble out of your pockets each time you leave home. If you set and follow a budget, you'll never again ask yourself, "Where did all my money go?"

A budget is simply a list of all your expenses compared with all your sources of income. You figure out what your monthly living expenses are and then decide what to do with any money left over. If there's nothing left over, that's OK. A budget is flexible. You can make changes, increasing some items and cutting others, until you find a formula that works for you.

When budgets don't work, it's usually because they're unrealistic (you swear you'll never go to the movies or go out to dinner again) or overly restrictive (a diet that doesn't allow you to eat any of your favorite foods is sure to fail), or because people simply abandon the budget when they feel frustrated about having to deny themselves something. But remember—the main reason for setting a budget is to rein in your spending so that you can pay off your debt and improve your credit.

Your expenses fall into two categories: fixed and discretionary. Fixed expenses are those that don't change from month to month, such as your rent or mortgage. Discretionary expenses change, depending on how much you choose to spend—say, on clothes or entertainment. When you write down all the places where you spend money, you might be surprised by how much money gets wasted on unimportant items that you could easily live without. With a little luck, you'll find some items in your budget that you can easily cut back on without significantly changing your lifestyle. (You can then take that money and send it off to your creditors to lower your debt.)

To set an accurate budget, start by taking out your checkbook and gathering all the receipts you can find. You probably haven't saved all your receipts, so for the next

two or three months, collect receipts from every purchase—even a pack of gum. When you think you have
everything, fill out a chart like the one on page 34. Eliminate the categories you don't need, and add any others
that pertain to your spending habits.

If you're computer-savvy, consider using a software program such as Microsoft Money or Quicken, or online
services such as Mvelopes (www.mvelopes.com). They do
basically the same thing as a handwritten budget chart,
but the programs do some of the math for you and can
help you project how your budget will change when you
alter your spending patterns. You can do the same kind of
analysis with a piece of paper, though. You certainly don't
need a computer to keep track of a budget.

As you start to track your spending, you should sit
down once a week and look at where the money is going.
This will help reinforce your new behavior and get you
into some good habits. After a few months, you can give
up the weekly analysis and do only a monthly one.

Next, take a look at your pay stubs from the past few
months. Tally up your monthly take-home income, after
income taxes and other deductions are taken out of your
check. If your take-home pay varies from month to
month, add up a year's worth and divide by 12 to get your
average monthly income.

Then, subtract your expenses from your income. If you
have money left over, that's great news. You can immediately increase what you send to your creditors each
month. But if you have a negative number, that means
you're buying things you can't pay for. You're going to
have some hard work ahead of you.

Get your list of needs and wants, and sit down with it
and your budget. Start with the budget items marked as
fixed. Some of these won't easily change, such as your

BUDGET CHART

Category	Fixed or Discretionary	Payment
HOUSING		
Mortgage or rent		$
Second mortgage/home equity loans		$
Property taxes		$
Homeowner's/renter's insurance		$
Condo fees		$
Association dues		$
Maintenance and repairs		$
UTILITIES		
Heating		$
Water		$
Electricity		$
Cable or satellite TV		$
Telephone		$
Cellular		$
Internet		$
Trash collection		$
FOOD		
Groceries		$
Meals out		$
Snacks (coffee, candy, mints, etc.)		$
CHILD CARE		
Day care		$
Babysitting		$
Child support		$
EDUCATION		
Tuition		$
School loans		$
Books and other supplies		$
Tutors		$
PERSONAL CARE		
Clothes		$
Toiletries (makeup, creams, hair care, etc.)		$
Laundry and dry cleaning		$
CREDIT		
Bank credit cards		$
Store and gasoline credit cards		$
Other loans		$

Category	Fixed or Discretionary	Payment
TRANSPORTATION		
Car payments		$
Gas, commuting, parking		$
Insurance, taxes, inspection		$
Repairs and maintenance		$
HEALTH		
Insurance payments		$
Doctors' bills not covered by insurance		$
Prescriptions		$
Eye care		$
Dental care		$
OTHER INSURANCE		
Life		$
Disability		$
Long-term care		$
ENTERTAINMENT		
Newspapers, magazines, books, movies		$
Books, DVDs, CDs, videos (purchases and rentals)		$
Hobbies and sports (equipment, clothing, etc.)		$
Vacations		$
Cigarettes		$
Alcohol		$
Lottery/casinos/bingo		$
MISCELLANEOUS		
Charity		$
Pets (food and care)		$
Gifts (holidays, birthdays, anniversaries)		$
SAVINGS		
401(k) plan		$
College fund		$
Other investments		$
Bank account		$
TOTAL EXPENSES:		$

rent. But maybe you can reduce your cable television bill. Do you really need the premium package? Do you need cable at all?

Now look at the discretionary items on your budget. This is where you'll have the most opportunity to save money. Have you been spending hundreds of dollars on wants, such as new clothes or nights out at the movies? You could cut back considerably here, and probably without much effort. How about your food category? If you eat out a lot, consider brown-bagging your lunch. If you save $6 a day on lunch money, 5 days a week, for 50 weeks, you'll save $1,500 a year. Or give up a coffee habit that's costing you $1 a day. Not very exciting, maybe, but the savings will be.

Circle the items you could eliminate, or reduce, and redo the math. You should have a lot more money left over after this initial round of cutbacks.

Again, don't think of this budget as a pair of handcuffs. It's a tool. It's going to empower you to get the things you really want—zero credit card balances, positive changes in your credit history, and the ability to plan for future goals without falling into financial quicksand.

SHOP SMARTER

As you adjust to life on a budget, you're going to have to learn to shop smarter. Here are some tips and strategies to help you become a clever consumer.

• Think, think, and think some more: Before you make a purchase, take some time to think about it. And that doesn't mean thinking while you're waiting on line for an available cashier. If you see something you want, take note of the price and walk away. When you're at home, away from the pressure of the store, think about whether the item is a want or a need. If it's a want, ask yourself how much you want it, and if it's worth paying less on your credit cards this month because you had to own it. If you decide you really must buy it, at least wait for a sale. Shop around. Compare prices. Find the best deal you can before you spend your money.

• Cash, cash, and more cash: If you can't pay cash for an item, forget it. No plastic. No more debt.

• Check your budget again: Suppose that the item you want is a jacket that costs $75. If you've budgeted only $25 a month for clothes, you'll have to wait three months before you can afford the jacket—and then you shouldn't buy anything else.

• Make a list and check it twice: When you go shopping, make a list of what you intend to buy, and stick to it. Buying unplanned items will bust your budget. These un-scheduled impulse purchases aren't going to help you reach your long-term financial goals.

• Buy in bulk: You can save substantial money when you buy everyday items in bulk. For example, most families use paper towels. At a store I went to recently, a single roll of paper towels cost $1.39. But if you bought a package of 15 rolls for $15.99, you'd pay only $1.07 a roll. That's a saving of 32 cents per roll, or $4.80 for the 15 rolls. You might ask, What's five bucks? Well, if you can find similar savings on other items you buy regularly, you'll significantly lower your grocery bill.

• Shop online: Some online stores have better prices than local shops. Because these companies don't have a store-front, they have a lower cost of doing business and they can pass the savings on to you, the consumer, in the form of lower prices. But remember—if you find a great deal, don't click your order until you find out the cost of shipping. The cost to ship your items could bring the total price up to a higher amount than the items cost in a local store.

STEP 4

NEGOTIATE WITH YOUR CREDITORS

Most consumers have credit cards with very high interest rates. In fact, the rates are so high that, added to your balance, they make it hard, if not impossible, to get ahead. It doesn't have to be that way. You can create a payment plan so that you don't have to file for bankruptcy and so that you don't have to continue paying skyrocketing interest rates.

Your creditors want their money. They don't want you to go belly-up and be unable to pay them back. There are plenty of moves you can make to create a more affordable debt load for yourself, all while giving your creditors the confidence that they'll see their money—slowly but surely.

WHY BANKRUPTCY ISN'T AN OPTION

Personal bankruptcies have been increasing for years. According to the most recent statistics available, there were more than 1.75 million personal bankruptcies filed in the 12-month period ending September 30, 2005. The American Bankruptcy Institute reports that this figure was up 10.4 percent from the year before.

You don't have to add yourself to that number, and you shouldn't. Although bankruptcy can clear out your debt, it will leave a black mark on your credit report. Recovering from that black mark would take you 7 to 10 years.

As of October 17, 2005, there were some changes in the bankruptcy law that make it harder to qualify for bankruptcy. Under the new law, before filing for bankruptcy a person must get credit counseling from a government-approved program. (To find an approved agency in your area, go to www.usdoj.gov/ust, and in the section called "Bankruptcy Reform" click on Credit Counseling and Debtor Education. Or visit the Esperanza Web site for a link.) The person in debt (the debtor) must stay in counseling for 180 days. The counseling process is supposed to help debtors figure out if they really need to file for bankruptcy, or if they can come up with another plan to pay off their debts. And once the bankruptcy case is over, debtors must go into counseling again, this time to learn budgeting. When debtors can prove they've attended the required counseling, the court will officially give them a bankruptcy discharge, which wipes the slate clean (if they file for Chapter 7—as explained below).

Before you even consider this step—and you really should abandon the idea completely—it's important to understand how bankruptcy works and what the consequences are.

HOW BANKRUPTCY WORKS

There are two types of bankruptcy for individuals: Chapter 7 and Chapter 13. (The word "chapter" refers to a section of the federal bankruptcy laws.)

Under Chapter 7, most of the amounts the debtor owes are discharged, or canceled. (But alimony and child support payments aren't included.) The debtor may have to give up some assets, depending on state law. Declaring Chapter 7 can also affect your insurance rating, your ability to rent an apartment, and your eligibility for some jobs.

Under Chapter 13, debts are not discharged but instead reorganized. This arrangement is for debtors who have too much disposable income to qualify for a Chapter 7 bankruptcy.

To determine which kind of bankruptcy you might qualify for, you have to pass a means test. This test looks at your average monthly income in the six months before filing, minus expenses for items such as transportation, food, monthly payments you make on secured debts (such as a mortgage or a car loan), and so-called priority debts such as alimony and child support. This leaves you with the amount of disposable income you have each month. If you have less than $100 of disposable income a month, you pass the means test and can file for Chapter 7. If your disposable income is greater than $166.66, you have to file for Chapter 13. If you're between these two amounts, you have another calculation to make. If after paying living expenses and secured debts, you have enough left over to pay 25 percent of your unsecured (credit card), nonpriority debts over five years, you can't file for Chapter 7.

Chapter 7

Filing under Chapter 7 generally takes four to six months and costs about $200 (for court fees) if you're not using a lawyer. To start the process, you'd have to fill out a bunch of forms about your debts, your assets, your income, and other items; and then you'd bring them to your local bankruptcy court.

Once you file, the people and companies to which you owe money are put on hold. This is called "automatic stay." (Evictions; lawsuits over paternity, custody, and child support; divorce proceedings; and lawsuits involving domestic violence are not included in the automatic stay.) Automatic stay means that creditors can't go after you for their money until your bankruptcy case is out of court. (And if you successfully declare bankruptcy, they'll never be able to go after you again.)

During this time, the court takes legal control of your

property (except for some items, which are exempt). You can't sell anything or pay any debts without the court's approval. The court will appoint a "bankruptcy trustee," whose job it is to make sure that as many of your debts as possible are paid. The trustee will go through what you own and what you owe in a court hearing called the "creditor's meeting." After this, any of your property that could be sold to pay your debts would be collected by the trustee. Usually, however, the trustee determines that most property either is not worth enough to sell or would be too difficult to sell. For example, a trustee wouldn't take a closetful of clothes or kitchen wares to sell to pay your debts but could take your stereo system, if he or she thinks it's worth selling. (Exactly what trustees will take depends on the state in which you live. Some states allow you to keep household goods and even wedding and engagement rings; others don't.)

If you don't want to lose a home or a car on which you still owe money—so-called secure debt, because the property is collateral, meaning that the creditor can take the property if you don't pay—you have to stay current with payments. You can usually make arrangements during the bankruptcy proceeding to keep the property as long as you keep paying.

Chapter 13

Chapter 13 bankruptcy is more of a reorganization of debt than a wiping out of what you owe.

You file forms similar to what you'd file for Chapter 7, but you include a suggested plan for how you can repay what you owe over a three- or five-year period. During this time, collections will be put on hold while the court proceedings continue. As with Chapter 7, you have a bankruptcy trustee. If your plan is accepted, you pay the trustee directly, and the trustee will make sure your creditors are paid.

One advantage of Chapter 13 over Chapter 7 is that it's gentler on your credit score. With Chapter 13, creditors see that you're making an effort to pay your debts. By contrast, with Chapter 7 your debts are erased and creditors generally receive nothing.

But erasing Chapter 13 from your credit report takes longer. A bankruptcy lingers on your credit report for 7 to 10 years. With Chapter 13, that 7- to 10-year period doesn't start until after you've paid your debts. So if it's going to take 5 years to pay, you will have that bankruptcy in your file for a minimum of 12 years.

Before you take the extreme step of filing for bankruptcy, there are many strategies you can try to pay your debt.

LET'S MAKE A DEAL

If you're having trouble paying your debts, creditors may be able to help. They want to be repaid their money, and they don't want to see you file for bankruptcy. If you file, they may never get back the money you borrowed.

The interest charged on the money you owe is probably making your debt grow, and creditors know this. They may be willing to change the terms of your account to help you get control. You have the best chance of negotiating a better deal if you haven't missed payments yet. If you're already behind, negotiating might be a bigger challenge, but it's still not impossible.

You need to start by being honest. Call your creditors and share your situation. Explain why you're having trouble meeting your obligations, and stress to them that you want to pay them back. If they believe you have good intentions, there's a very good chance they'll offer to help.

And be polite. People are more likely to help you if you treat them with respect, even when you don't agree with what they're saying.

Before you call, you need to know what you can afford to pay. It makes no sense to agree on a deal that you won't be able to uphold. The creditor will never trust you in the future if you don't keep your word. Examining your budget and your overall debt as discussed in previous chapters will show you what you can afford to pay.

Tell the creditors how much you can afford to pay and how long it will take to pay the debt. There are different offers creditors might make. They may agree to lower your interest rate, or they might stop charging you interest altogether, as long as you make steady payments on your balance. They may settle for a smaller payment than the entire balance you owe, if you can pay it up front. Or they may be willing to negotiate another kind of payment plan.

Some debts are easier to negotiate than others. You probably won't be able to get anywhere with a mortgage company, but credit card companies negotiate better deals all the time. They want to keep you as a customer, and because it's unsecured debt, they won't get anything if you can't pay. (By contrast, you could lose a home or a car if you default on a mortgage or a car loan.) If creditors have to hand your account to a collection agency, it will cost them more money. It's better for them to deal directly with you.

Make sure you keep records of who you spoke to, when you had the conversation, and what was said. After you call and speak to the creditor, send a follow-up letter reminding the person what was agreed to.

It's possible that no matter how hard you try, your creditors won't make a deal with you. If this happens, try again in writing. Explain in your letter the extent of all your debts and your income, and show your payment plan in writing. Here's a sample of what you might send:

Date
Your Name
Your Address
Your City, State, Zip Code

Complaint Department
Name of Company
Address
City, State, Zip Code

Dear Sir or Madam:
I am having trouble meeting my debt obligations, and I would like to propose a payment plan to you.
I (explain why you are having trouble making payments, such as a job loss, etc.), but I want to meet my obligations. On (insert date here), I spoke with (insert name here) of your company, and we were unable to reach a payment agreement. I'm hoping you'll reconsider.
I earn (your income here) per year, and my total debt is (list debts here). My expenses for (list rent or mortgage and other necessary expenses here) total (say how much these expenses are each month). Because I do not want to default on this account, I propose (add your payment ideas here).
I appreciate your attention to this matter, and thank you for helping me meet my debt obligation to you.

Sincerely,
Your name

You may not get a positive response on your first try. But be persistent. Politely ask to speak to supervisors or people in higher positions with the company. If you're patient and determined, you'll have a better chance at success.

RESPONDING TO DEBT COLLECTORS

If you haven't been paying your debts at all, it's possible that a creditor will go to a debt collection service. This service will try to collect from you the money you owe. But such a service is not allowed to harass you. In fact, there are laws governing how a debt collector may approach you for a payment.

You need to understand what debt collectors can and can't do. Because laws vary widely from state to state, you need to find out what applies in your area. To get contact information for the attorney general's office in your state, call 202-326-6000 or go online to www.naag.org. This link is also available on the Esperanza Web site.

The National Consumer Law Center offers a free brochure, "What You Should Know about Debt Collection." Call 617-542-9595 to ask for a copy, or go to www.nclc.org. The Federal Trade Commission (www.ftc.gov) also has a free brochure about debt collection, or call 877-FTC-HELP to get a copy. These links are also available on the Esperanza Web site.

Essentially, debt collectors are allowed to contact you by mail, telephone, or fax, or in person. They may not contact you before 8 a.m. or after 9 p.m. without your consent. They also cannot contact you at work if you've told them not to. They cannot tell other people, including your employer or neighbors, about the collection. They may not threaten you with violence or arrest or say that they will garnish your wages (unless the creditor is actually taking steps to do so).

Within five days of first contacting you, collectors must give you some information in writing. They must tell you how much money you owe, to whom you owe it, and what you can do if you disagree that you owe any money.

Once debt collectors have contacted you, you can tell them to stop. Send a letter to them, telling them to stop. Then, they can't contact you except to tell you about any actions the creditor is planning to take.

You can negotiate with a debt collector just as you can with any other creditor. Use the ideas discussed earlier in this chapter to negotiate a payment plan or some other payoff strategy. But before you start paying, make sure you have something in writing from the collectors stating exactly what the agreement is. Have them state, also, that they will contact the credit bureaus to explain the details of your agreement.

Unfortunately, any collection will stay on your credit report for seven years. So make sure the terms of your agreement and the proof that you're paying appear on your credit report.

After you've made a deal, you can ask the debt collector to remove any negative information from your credit report. You may not succeed, but it never hurts to ask. Also ask that when your debt is paid, your account will show you have a zero balance. This will show you paid your debt in full.

IF YOU'RE FACING EVICTION

Eviction is the legal proceeding through which you are removed from your rented property. This is bad news for you, the tenant. But it's not pretty for a landlord, either.

Landlords don't like evictions, because they cost money. Landlords may need to hire costly attorneys, and afterward they're left with an empty property for which they have to find a new tenant. Also, the laws often favor tenants, to ensure that no one is thrown out onto the street overnight.

If you're unable to pay your rent, contact your landlord right away. A landlord may be willing to agree to a payment plan if you show the ability to pay what you owe in the future. If you can't come to an agreement, local laws will govern what happens next.

To learn about eviction laws in your community, go to the legal Web site FindLaw.com (www.findlaw.com). At this link, which is also available on the Esperanza Web site, you can find eviction laws state by state: http://realestate.find law.com/tenant/tenant-resources/tenant-state-laws.html.

Before you are evicted, generally speaking, a landlord must give you written notice that you have breached your rental contract, and the landlord must tell you what you must do—such as making a payment—to stop an eviction process in the courts. The landlord may not threaten you physically and may not threaten to remove you from the property, or change the locks, or shut off the heat, and so on.

The landlord will then go to court, and you and the landlord will tell the judge your sides of the story. If the landlord wins, the court will issue an eviction order, which allows the landlord to have local law enforcement remove you and your property from the rental property. This can take time, as local law enforcement often has more pressing matters and a long list of evictions before yours.

The eviction may appear on your credit report, as the results of the eviction case will be available as part of public court documents.

STEP 5

PAY
ON TIME

It sounds simple. Pay your bills on time, and you'll rebuild your credit report and have your finances under control. But if you're having money troubles, it's easier said than done.

Paying on time is the only way to rebuild trust with creditors and the credit bureaus. It's more important to pay on time than it is to pay your credit card in full. The credit card companies don't mind if you keep a balance (that's how they make money—on the interest they charge you). But they do mind if they don't get paid on time.

Paying late will mean higher fees, higher interest rates, and eventually negative reports from your lender to the credit bureaus.

Although you may feel somewhat trapped by your credit card debt, remember that you're the customer. If you feel that you're not being treated fairly, you can shop around for better deals. Of course, any card company will want customers to stick to their agreements by making timely payments. So that's where we'll start.

SET YOURSELF UP FOR SUCCESS

We've already talked about how interest rates are calculated by credit card companies. But there's a lot more to how credit cards work than interest rates. It's important to understand what other fees you can face if you're not paying on time.

First, you should know that if a payment is a few days late, the credit card company isn't going to report you to the credit bureaus. Payments usually have to be more than 30 days late before the bureaus are notified. But payments that are a just few days late can still cost you money.

Credit cards impose "late fees" for payments that don't come in on time. These fees can be as high as $39. Even utilities like your gas or electric company or insurance companies may have fees for late payments. Different lenders have different fee structures, as stated in the contract you received when you first got a credit card or signed up with a utility or other company. Few consumers save these contracts, so if you're not sure what yours says about fees and other specifics, call the 800 number on the back of your card or on your bill and ask for a new copy. Much of the information you'll want to know will also be printed on the back of your monthly bill.

By law, credit card companies must credit payments to your account on the same day these payments are received. If you don't follow the company's guidelines for payment, the company is permitted to take up to five days to process your payment, and payment could then be considered late.

You should also understand that your credit card contract probably says it can substantially increase your interest rate if your payment is late. So not only will you pay a late fee; you'll also be charged higher interest.

Most lenders also have a so-called grace period. A grace period is the time between when the bill is sent to you and when your payment is due. During the grace period—generally between 20 and 30 days from the time the lender sends you the bill—the lender doesn't charge you interest while it waits for your payment. But if you are already running a balance by not paying in full each month, the grace period won't apply to your account.

There are some steps you can take to make sure your payment gets there on time and follows the company's guidelines.

Start by always using the payment coupon and the envelope the company sends you with your bill. Write the amount you're paying on the payment coupon and write your account number on the check.

If you make minimum payments, you've probably noticed that your minimums are higher than they used to be. Most credit cards used to calculate your minimum payment as 2 percent of your balance. Although paying the minimum right away is wise, so that your payment is on time, you'll have to pay more to get rid of your debt in a reasonable time. We discussed in Step 2 how a credit card with a balance of $2,000 at 15 percent interest will take 264 months, or 22 years, to pay off if you pay only the minimum. That's a long time. That $2,000 balance credit card would have a minimum payment of $40. That 2 percent would pay interest and fees, and very little toward your purchases. But now, credit card companies are requiring that you pay higher minimums. Though it may hurt your wallet to be required to pay more, it's actually for your own good. Here's why.

Federal banking regulators—the Office of the Comptroller of the Currency, a bureau of the U.S. Treasury Department—issued new guidelines to credit card companies, effective October 2005, saying that minimum payments should cover interest, fees, and at least 1 percent of the principal (the purchases you've made). This has probably doubled your minimum payment from 2 percent to 4 percent of your outstanding balance.

The idea behind the 4 percent minimum (instead of a 2 percent minimum) is that it will help consumers pay off their debt much faster. Instead of 264 months, you'll pay it off in 105 months. You'll pay significantly less interest over time, too.

ORGANIZE YOUR PAYMENTS

In Step 2, we talked about creating a chart that lists all your debts. The chart included due dates. When you use the chart, you might be tempted to wait until you're close to a due date to make the payment. If you want to ensure that you're never late, consider sending the minimum payment on the day you receive the bill. (Or allot one day a week for paying bills, and pay the minimum then.) If you have more money available to send later in the month, you can always make another payment in the middle of the month. But you need to at least send the minimum so you're not hit with a late fee.

If you find that too many of your bills are due on the same date, or during the same time of the month, you can call the lenders and ask if they'll change your date. For example, if you have three credit cards that are always due around the fifteenth of the month, ask that one of them be changed to the first of the month.

If you have a computer, consider using an online bill paying service. Many banks offer this service free. Instead of writing the check yourself, you can tell your bank when to make payments, and how much to send. You'll set up a payment calendar similar to the one you can create by hand. Many lenders will gladly accept electronic payments, though others don't. You can still make online payments to those who don't: for those, your bank will cut the check and mail it so that you don't have to.

If, despite these steps, you still find you're going to be late with a payment, call the lender and see if it will give you a one-time extension on the due date. This could save you the late-payment fee.

You also have the option of paying by phone if you're afraid the payment will get there late. Simply call the credit card company and give it your checking account number and the bank routing number, which is found on the lower left-hand side of your check. (The routing number is what financial institutions use to wire money.) Most lenders will charge a fee for a phone payment, and this fee could be as high as $25 for a one-time payment. That is costly, indeed, but it might be cheaper than the late fee and the higher interest you could be charged if your payment doesn't get there on time.

Another option is to send the payment by overnight mail through the post office, or overnight by another delivery service, such as FedEx or Airborne Express. You'll have to pay for these services, too, so weigh the cost against the fees you might be charged on your credit card.

WHO'S HELPING WHOM?

Sometimes you might feel like a victim of your credit cards, or you might feel as if a company is doing you a favor by letting you use its card. But in reality, you are doing the credit card company a favor, by giving it your business and helping it make money. You have the power to make your own decisions about whom you're going to do business with. Companies need you more than you need them.

Credit card companies couldn't stay in business if they didn't have customers. True, many of these companies are huge, with thousands of employees and even more customers. Would they care if you weren't a customer anymore?

Of course they would. Customer service representatives are instructed to be polite, to try to help you when you call, and—most important—to do whatever they can to keep you as a customer. There are thousands of credit cards available for consumers, and the credit card companies know this. If you're not happy with the service you're receiving, you'll go elsewhere with your business.

If your credit is less than perfect, now may not be the best time to start shopping for new credit. Instead, work to get better deals on the cards you already have.

If you have a high interest rate, call your company and ask if it can lower your rate. Tell it you have a better offer. (Go to BankRate.com, and you'll certainly find a more competitive offer. The credit card companies know what their competition is offering.) You should say something like this:

> Hello, this is [your name]. I've been receiving a lot of offers in the mail for credit cards with low interest rates. I'm tempted to take one. Can you give me a better deal?

There's a good chance, if your account is in good standing, that the lender will lower your rate a few points. If your payments haven't been on time lately, you'll have less leverage, but you can always try to negotiate.

USING CREDIT CARDS WISELY

No matter how much credit you have available to you—and you'll have a lot, once you pay off your outstanding debts—you have to apply self-control when it comes to using your credit cards.

Credit cards can be a fantastic tool. They give you some protections if you buy a defective product or have a dispute with a merchant. They're also convenient, and you don't have to worry about how much cash you have in your pocket before you go shopping. But you do have to worry about how much cash you have in the bank. If you can't pay for your purchases in full when the monthly statement comes in, don't buy. Wait. Start a savings plan, which we'll talk about in Step 10, and then you'll be able to pay cash for the purchases you really want. Then you can really enjoy them, debt-free.

SHOPPING FOR THE BEST DEALS ON CREDIT CARDS

If you are ready to shop for new credit cards, the best tool out there is the BankRate.com Web site (www.bankrate.com). In addition to some great educational articles, the site offers a comprehensive search engine for credit card deals.

If you don't have a computer, this is a good reason to find one, even for an hour or two. Ask family members or friends, ask your employer, or visit your local library. It may also be worth paying a few dollars to use one of the computers at an Internet café. Ask around, and you're sure to find a place where you can use a computer for a short time.

When you're on the site, go to the credit card area. Here you'll find a list of calculators and articles, but the feature you want is the box at the upper left-hand side of the screen, which says, "Compare credit card offers and rates in just a few simple steps." Then you can choose the type of card you want to find:

• Low-interest cards: These cards have some of the lowest interest rates available.

• No-annual-fee cards: As the name implies, these charge no annual fee.

• Secured cards: These are cards for people who have had credit problems. You put a certain amount of money in an untouchable account with the lender, and the lender gives you a credit card with that same limit. The lender is taking no risk, because it already has your money in the bank in case you can't pay the credit card charges. These are good tools to reestablish credit and show you can make timely payments.

• Airline mile cards: These allow you to accumulate points or credit toward air travel.

• Rewards cards: These are cards that allow you to accumulate points toward different rewards, such as free or discounted products, money to use toward a car purchase, etc.

On the site, choose the kind of card you're looking for, and the site will give you a list of the best deals offered by banks around the country. On the list you'll find information about interest rates, fees, grace periods, and how to contact the lender.

Before you start shopping for new cards, here are a few points you'll want to consider.

• Low interest rates: It might seem obvious that the lowest interest rate is the best deal, but that's not always so. Many cards offer a very, very low introductory rate, called a teaser rate, that lasts for a short time, perhaps six months. Then after six months, that low rate shoots up to 22 percent or so, much higher than other cards on the market. For example, let's compare two cards: one with an introductory rate of 2.9 percent for the first six months and then a rate of 22 percent thereafter, versus one with a steady rate of 12 percent. Each has a $1,000 balance. Over two years, if you're paying the minimum on both cards, the balance on the card with the low introductory rate will be a shocking $15,976, all because of that huge 22 percent interest. The balance on the steady 12 percent

TEMPTING OFFER RATE

	Starting Balance	APR	Statement Balance	Minimum Payment	Ending Balance
Jan-06	1000	2.9%	1029.00	41.16	987.84
Feb-06		2.9%	1016.49	40.66	975.83
Mar-06		2.9%	1004.13	40.17	963.96
Apr-06		2.9%	991.92	39.68	952.24
May-06		2.9%	979.85	39.19	940.66
Jun-06		2.9%	967.94	38.72	929.22
Jul-06		22%	1133.65	45.35	1088.31
Aug-06		22%	1327.73	53.11	1274.62
Sep-06		22%	1555.04	62.20	1492.84
Oct-06		22%	1821.26	72.85	1748.41
Nov-06		22%	2133.06	85.32	2047.74
Dec-06		22%	2498.24	99.93	2398.31
Jan-07		22%	2925.94	117.04	2808.91
Feb-07		22%	3426.86	137.07	3289.79
Mar-07		22%	4013.54	160.54	3853.00
Apr-07		22%	4700.66	188.03	4512.64
May-07		22%	5505.42	220.22	5285.20
Jun-07		22%	6447.94	257.92	6190.03
Jul-07		22%	7551.83	302.07	7249.76
Aug-07		22%	8844.70	353.79	8490.92
Sep-07		22%	10358.92	414.36	9944.56
Oct-07		22%	12132.36	485.29	11647.07
Nov-07		22%	14209.42	568.38	13641.05
Dec-07		22%	16642.08	665.68	15976.40

LEVEL RATE

	APR	Statement Balance	Minimum Payment	Ending Balance
Jan-06	12%	1120.00	44.80	1075.20
Feb-06	12%	1204.22	48.17	1156.06
Mar-06	12%	1294.78	51.79	1242.99
Apr-06	12%	1392.15	55.69	1336.46
May-06	12%	1496.84	59.87	1436.97
Jun-06	12%	1609.40	64.38	1545.03
Jul-06	12%	1730.43	69.22	1661.21
Aug-06	12%	1860.56	74.42	1786.13
Sep-06	12%	2000.47	80.02	1920.45
Oct-06	12%	2150.91	86.04	2064.87
Nov-06	12%	2312.65	92.51	2220.15
Dec-06	12%	2486.57	99.46	2387.10
Jan-07	12%	2673.55	106.94	2566.61
Feb-07	12%	2874.61	114.98	2759.62
Mar-07	12%	3090.78	123.63	2967.15
Apr-07	12%	3323.20	132.93	3190.27
May-07	12%	3573.11	142.92	3430.18
Jun-07	12%	3841.81	153.67	3688.13
Jul-07	12%	4130.71	165.23	3965.48
Aug-07	12%	4441.34	177.65	4263.69
Sep-07	12%	4775.33	191.01	4584.31
Oct-07	12%	5134.43	205.38	4929.05
Nov-07	12%	5520.54	220.82	5299.72
Dec-07	12%	5935.69	237.43	5698.26

card will be $5,698. Either way, paying only the minimum is costly. But after that low introductory rate ends and the 22 percent rate kicks in, you're paying interest on the interest. It's called compound interest. As the interest charges are added to your balance, your balance grows, and you start getting charged interest on that entire balance—which includes interest charges that have already been attached to your account. This means that if you can't start paying significantly more than the minimum, you'll never catch up. That's what makes the debt load ridiculously high in a mere two years.

• Annual fees: Do you really want to pay an annual fee for the privilege of using a credit card? You'll already be paying interest on the money you borrow, if you're not able to pay in full. Choosing a card with a slightly higher interest rate but no annual fee will cost you less in the long run.

• Rewards cards: These may offer attractive rewards, but they also often have higher interest rates and higher annual fees. They're probably not worth the cost for most consumers.

• Your existing cards: You may get the best deal of all by negotiating with your current card companies. They'll want to keep you as a customer.

We'll talk about secured cards in Step 7.

STEP 6

PAY IT OFF

Paying your bills on time is critical to improving your credit report, but paying down your debt and taking steps to eliminate it will give you a feeling of even more freedom—plus that clean credit report.

Creditors will be pleased to see that you're not carrying huge balances, especially on credit cards (revolving debt). They'll be more likely to extend new credit if you don't already owe a ton of money. And credit scoring takes into account the amount of debt you're carrying compared with the amount of available credit you have. Your score will improve if you make progress here.

WHAT TO PAY FIRST?

With several creditors in line to get paid, you need to use smart strategies to decide who should be paid first. Of course, you can't concentrate completely on one debt, because you have to pay at least the minimums on your other bills. But you can come up with a priority list so you can send all your extra cash to one debt, eventually eliminating that debt completely. Then, you'll move on to the next one.

Before you establish a payoff plan, you need to think about what bills take priority. These are the bills for items you need in order to live—the ones that will keep your family's security and health intact.

By the way, I'm not suggesting you should intentionally

default on less important debts while you're concentrating on the necessities. You shouldn't skip a rent payment to pay a credit card bill, because being without a home is a far worse problem than credit card debt.

So, housing comes first. You need to stay current on your rent or your mortgage. If you don't, you could be without a place to live, and then—as I've just said—your credit card bills won't be your biggest problem anymore.

Next come your utilities. Bills from the gas company, the electric company, and the water company need to be paid. What's the sense in having a house or apartment if conditions there are unlivable because you don't have heat, water, or electricity? You can let telephone and cable bills slide if you have to (but you will have to pay them eventually). Though it may be hard to imagine living without them, telephone and cable services are technically luxury items.

You also need to stay on top of your needs for food and medical care. Doctors' bills you already owe aren't the priority, but you do need to make sure you meet payments for health insurance. You don't want to let your insurance policy lapse. Too many uninsured families end up in long-term financial trouble if they are hit with serious illness or injury.

Income taxes, child support, and alimony come next. If you don't pay these bills, you could go to jail. The IRS or the courts could decide to garnish your wages (take money from your paycheck before the check is paid to you) to make sure these items are paid. If you have a big unpaid tax bill, you can contact the IRS to design a payment plan. Call 800-829-1040 or visit www.irs.gov. (Or visit the Esperanza USA Web site at www.esperanza.us for a link.)

Once those bills are paid, you need to think hard about your car. If you have a loan or a lease, the lender could take back possession of the vehicle if you don't make your payments. If you have trouble making the payments, consider selling the car and buying a cheaper one. Or, if it's feasible (however uncomfortable), consider using mass transit instead. If you keep your car, stay current on auto insurance payments, too.

If you owe student loans, it's smart to stay current. Lenders can garnish your wages or even take your tax refunds for payment. Contact your lender to see if you can defer payments until sometime in the future, when you hope your finances will be more secure.

Next come your unsecured loans—your credit card debt. These can feel like the hardest to prioritize, but it's all a matter of dollars and cents.

Simply pay the debt with the highest interest rate first. The reason: the credit card with the highest interest rate is costing you the most money in fees and interest charges on a monthly basis. If you have three credit cards with three different interest rates—say 22 percent, 18 percent, and 15 percent—you should first pay off the one that charges 22 percent interest.

Some advisers suggest that instead of paying the card with the highest interest rate first, you should pay the card with the smallest balance. They say you'll feel great satisfaction in having a zero balance, and it might give you the incentive to keep paying down your debt. Of course you'll feel great when you pay off a bill, but if you don't attack first the ones with the highest interest rates, you're going to owe more money overall. (This assumes you've already stopped using your credit cards for new charges. If you're still charging as you're trying to pay off the debt, you'll only get frustrated.)

Keep in mind that all lenders feel as if the money you owe them is the most important. Don't allow threats from creditors to change your mind about who should be paid first. Once you establish a plan, stick to it. Of course, if you're getting threats from a creditor who can take away something you need, such as your home, you should pay special attention to what you owe that creditor. (In Step 4, we discussed how and when a creditor can contact you, and the moves you can take to stop any harassing contact.)

As we discussed with regard to good debt and bad debt in Step 2, mortgages are considered good debt. You shouldn't be in a rush to make extra payments on secured debts such as your home. Stay current, of course; but while you have a mortgage, you'll benefit by deducting the mortgage interest from your income tax. The biggest savings come when you pay down your high-interest credit cards.

CREDIT COUNSELING SERVICES AND DEBT CONSOLIDATION

If have can't seem to balance your bills, and negotiating directly with your creditors didn't have the results you'd hoped for, you may want to consider a nonprofit consumer credit counseling service. You'll pay for its services, but it carries more weight with a creditor than you do as an individual.

Consumer credit counseling services (CCCS) help you arrange payment plans (called debt management plans) with your creditors. Instead of paying your creditors directly, you'll make monthly payments to the service, and it will in turn pay your creditors.

Using a service like this is a big deal. Like a bankruptcy, it will stay on your credit report for seven years. For that reason, don't jump to this as an easy answer to your problems. It's more of a last resort.

Some companies that offer debt management services are very reputable. Others are not. For example, some take several months to negotiate with your creditors. This could be a problem, because these services often advise you to stop paying your creditors while the negotiating process takes place. If you've been making your payments on time and then suddenly stop on the advice of a debt service, you're going to add some bad marks to your credit report.

Dealing with CCCS will not necessarily eliminate your obligations to pay interest, but the service will try to negotiate so that interest charges are either halted or reduced, and it will ask for fees to be eliminated. Generally, debt repayment plans with CCCS last from three to five years. Your credit accounts will probably be suspended during this time, so you cannot make new charges.

If you use a CCCS, that fact will appear on your credit report. Creditors may mark "not being paid as agreed" on your report, and they may also report that they are receiving payments through a service instead of directly from you. After these notations appear on your credit report, it may take a few years before you're able to get new credit. The marks will stay on your report for seven years. The good news is that they will not have a bad effect on your credit score.

If you don't pick a reputable CCCS, and the one you choose makes late payments to your creditors, that will harm your credit. Payments will show as being late, and the fact that a service, not you, was late in making the payments won't help the situation. You may see a company advertise on television, and it may say it's a nonprofit, but that doesn't mean it's reputable. And remember that you might be best off simply calling your creditors yourself. That way, at least you'll know for certain where your payments are going, and you won't be paying extra fees to a middleman.

For help in choosing a credit counselor, check out the

FTC's brochure "Fiscal Fitness: Choosing a Credit Counselor." Call 877-FTC-HELP, visit www.ftc.gov, or find the link on the Esperanza site, at www.esperanza.us. Then visit the Web site for the National Foundation for Credit Counseling (www.nfcc.org), use the link on the Esperanza Web site, or call 800-388-2228 to find a counselor near you.

It's very important to shop around for a credit counselor, making sure the one you choose is reputable and that there are no consumer complaints against it. To check out a service, contact your local Better Business Bureau (in your phone book) or check online at their site, www.bbb.org (or find their link on the Esperanza USA Web site).

Make sure to ask for a written description of all the fees and charges before you sign on with anyone. These are nonprofit groups, but their services aren't free. There's no set fee you should expect. Some charge a small monthly fee. Others charge hundreds of dollars. Cheapest doesn't necessarily mean best, here. Make sure to shop around.

Watch out for groups that want a large amount of money as a down payment. This is where many credit counselors are engaging in fraud. They'll take a big chunk of cash from you up front, and use it for their fees instead of putting any of it toward your debt. And because your debt isn't being paid, this can put you and your credit in even worse shape.

Whichever CCCS you hire, you want to make sure it treats you with respect and gives you some real services. It should be willing to help you create a budget and teach you about using credit—and to spend more than five minutes with you. Not everyone with credit trouble has the same problems, and you want the counselor to look at your specific situation before giving out any advice.

The Federal Trade Commission (FTC) wants consumers to ask these questions, as published on the FTC Web site.

• *What services do you offer?* Look for an organization that offers a range of services, including budget counseling, classes on savings and debt management, and counselors who are trained and certified in consumer credit, money and debt management, and budgeting. Counselors should discuss your entire financial situation with you, and help you develop a personalized plan to solve your money problems now and avoid others in the future. An initial counseling session typically lasts an hour, with an offer of follow-up sessions. Avoid organizations that push a debt management plan as your only option before they spend a significant amount of time analyzing your financial situation. Debt management programs (DMPs) are not for everyone. You should sign up for a DMP only after a certified credit counselor has spent time thoroughly reviewing your financial situation, and has offered you customized advice on managing your money. If you were on a DMP with an organization that closed down, ask any credit counselors that you are considering what they can do to help you retain the benefits of your DMP.

• *Are you licensed to offer your services in my state?* Many states require that an organization register or obtain a license before offering credit counseling, debt management plans, and similar services. Do not hire an organization that has not fulfilled the requirements for your state.

• *Do you offer free information?* Avoid organizations that charge for information about the nature of their services.

• *Will I have a formal written agreement or contract with you?* Don't commit yourself to participate in a DMP over the telephone. Get all promises in writing. Read all documents carefully before you sign them. If you are told you need to act immediately, consider finding another organization.

• *What are the qualifications of your counselors? Are they accredited or certified by an outside organization? If so, which one? If not, how are they trained?* Try to use an organization whose counselors are trained by an outside organization that is not affiliated with creditors.

- *Have other consumers been satisfied with the service that they received?* Once you've identified credit counseling organizations that suit your needs, check them out with your state attorney general, local consumer protection agency, and Better Business Bureau. These sources can tell you if consumers have filed complaints about a credit counseling service. An absence of complaints doesn't guarantee legitimacy, but complaints from other consumers may alert you to problems.

- *What are your fees? Are there setup and/or monthly fees?* Get a detailed price, quoted in writing, and specifically ask whether all the fees are covered in the quote. If you're concerned that you cannot afford to pay your fees, ask if the organization waives or reduces fees when providing counseling to consumers in your circumstances. If an organization won't help you because you can't afford to pay, look elsewhere for help.

- *How are your employees paid? Are the employees paid more, or is the organization paid more, if I sign up for certain services, pay a fee, or make a contribution to your organization?* Employees who are counseling you to purchase certain services may receive a commission if you choose to sign up for those services. Many credit counseling organizations receive additional compensation from creditors if you enroll in a DMP. If the organization will not disclose what compensation it receives from creditors, or how employees are compensated, go elsewhere for help.

- *What do you do to keep personal information about your clients (for example, name, address, phone number, and financial information) confidential and secure?* Credit counseling organizations handle your most sensitive financial information. The organization should have safeguards in place to protect the privacy of this information and prevent misuse.

SHOULD I TRANSFER MY CREDIT CARD BALANCES?

One tempting way to eliminate credit cards with high interest rates is to move the balance to a card with a low rate or zero rate. This may seem as if it will save you money, but it's something you should approach with caution.

Moving debt around instead of paying it off won't help your credit score. In fact, it will hurt your score. MyFico.com says that owing smaller amounts on several different credit card accounts can lower your score more than having a high balance on just one card. Also, some zero-interest cards aren't as good a deal as they seem. Most offer these low rates for a set time period, anywhere from 6 to 18 months or longer. But when the low rate expires, your remaining balance will be subject to a higher interest rate—sometimes well over 20 percent. In that case, you're saving in the short run; but if you don't have a plan to pay down your debt, you're only delaying the inevitable.

And each time you transfer a balance, you'll pay a fee, often as high as 4 percent of the balance you're moving. Plus, you need to be careful about the terms of your new card. If you make a late payment, often the interest rate will skyrocket on your entire balance and you'll be back where you started. Some of these cards also require you to make a certain minimum of new purchases using the card to qualify for the low interest rate. If you don't, you'll lose the rate. (You don't want to be adding to your credit card debt now, either.)

And if you move balances several times, you're going to have a bunch of unused (I hope unused) credit cards, giving you a substantial credit line when you add them all together. This can scare off future lenders, because on paper, you have the ability to charge too much too fast with all your available credit.

At the same time, closing unused cards won't necessarily help you, either. If you close an old account, you're going to shorten your credit history, and that could mean a lower credit score. And you won't erase negative information about that account anytime soon. Late payments and other negative items with that account will stay on your report for a while. You're better off keeping your oldest cards, as long as you can resist the temptation to use them. (Of course, if you have five cards, each with an annual fee of $75, you could be wasting $375 a year.)

If you do close an account, you want the lender to note on your report that the account was closed at your request. That way it won't look as if the lender decided not to stay in business with you.

One last note on balance transfers. If you're a home owner, you might be tempted to use a home equity loan or a home equity line of credit to pay off your debt. These loans allow you to borrow against the value of your home. They offer interest rates that are generally lower than other loans, and the interest payments on these loans are generally tax-deductible. Despite the advantages, you should consider these loans with caution. You're essentially putting your home on the line. If you default on a home equity loan or line of credit payments, you're putting your house at risk as collateral. The bank could take your home if you don't pay. It's probably not worth the risk.

There's no one right or easy answer. Just consider all the possibilities before deciding on a new borrowing option for your existing debt.

STEP 7

ADD POSITIVE INFORMATION TO YOUR FILE

After you've faced your credit problems and you've started making arrangements for paying what you owe, it's time to start adding positive information to your credit file.

Whether you've negotiated with your creditors, turned to a credit counseling service, or declared bankruptcy, the way you manage credit from this point forward will show lenders that you've gotten serious about improving your credit.

As we've already discussed, making timely payments and attempting to pay off your balances will start to improve your credit score. But there are other ways you can add good news for lenders.

MANAGE THE CREDIT YOU HAVE

If you declared bankruptcy or if you used a debt management program, you probably can't continue to use your old credit card accounts. These accounts were or will be closed after the balances are paid or discharged.

But if you still have credit cards, you can work with your existing accounts to establish a positive payment pattern on future charges.

First, remember the lessons you've learned about budgets. Keep in mind how much you can afford to spend before you buy anything on credit. If you can't pay your card in full at the end of the month, don't buy—don't add to your debt.

But to show good payment habits to your lenders, you're going to have to charge something and then pay it off. Not using a card (however wise that may be) will not increase your credit score. Instead, charge a small item—say, something costing $20, or whatever you can afford—and then pay your bill in full when it's due. Or charge something you were going to buy anyway, something that's already part of your budget, such as your groceries or gasoline for your car. Lenders will see that you're making timely payments, and you won't be adding to your existing debt.

You may have high credit limits—the amount a lender will allow you to charge—on your existing cards, and that can be too tempting. Call each of your card companies and request a lower credit limit. How much? That depends on what you can afford to pay each month. If you can afford only $50 or $100, ask for your limit to be lowered to that amount, or set only slightly higher.

But before you call, set aside your credit card with the highest credit limit and save it for emergencies. Once you have a zero balance on this card, freeze it or stick it under your mattress. This will take some discipline, but you should never use this card except for serious financial emergencies. Use another card with a lower balance for your day-to-day spending.

In the future, as your positive credit history grows and you show lenders you can pay your debts on time, you can always ask for an increased credit limit on your other cards.

APPLY FOR A SECURED CREDIT CARD

If you've declared bankruptcy, or if you've put your future payments in the hands of a debt management program with a credit counseling service, all your current accounts are likely to be closed. That means you need to establish new credit—which of course, can be hard to do, given your recent history.

One of the best ways to establish new credit is with a secured credit card. A secured card is a credit card that's secured or backed by a deposit you make into a savings account. The funds in this savings account aren't there for you to spend. Instead, they are collateral on the secured credit card.

A lender will give you a line of credit based on the amount of money you have in the account. Sometimes your credit line will be equal to the amount you deposit, but sometimes it will be just a percentage of your balance. Different secured cards have different deposit requirements, generally ranging from $250 to $500, and you'll earn interest on this money. How much credit you get, and the interest rate your deposit earns, will vary from lender to lender.

This is an easy risk for the lender. If you don't pay back the money you owe on the secured credit card, the lender keeps the money you deposited into the bank account. Still, the lender wants to make money on your account. As with a traditional credit card, you will owe interest on any charges that you're not able to pay in full when your bill is due. If you don't pay, the lender's decision to take the money in the savings account instead is not reached lightly, but you can further damage your credit if you don't make payments. So, simply make the payments and don't overcharge.

Secured cards can be helpful for several reasons. If you were having a hard time limiting your spending with traditional credit cards, a secured card will have a relatively small limit. And everyone needs a credit card sometimes. It's hard to rent a car or a hotel room without one—and if because of your past credit mistakes you no longer qualify for traditional credit cards, a secured card will serve the same purpose. Merchants won't know the difference when they see the card.

When you shop for a secured card, make sure you're getting the least costly card possible. Some cards will have fees costing hundreds of dollars, but you can find a far better deal. Of course, a no-fee card is best, but you can expect most cards to charge an annual fee between $20 and $35. Some will also want to charge so-called setup fees or registration fees, while others won't. A small one-time charge is reasonable, but if the card company is asking for a lot of money, look around for a better deal.

Next, take a close look at the interest rate and the overall contract. Interest rates will vary, often on the basis of your credit history. A search for secured cards on the Web site BankRate.com yielded cards ranging from a low of 8.9 percent to a high of 22.24 percent. Read contracts to make sure the cards have grace periods, reasonable late fees, and reasonable over-the-limit fees; and understand what will happen to your account if you default on a payment.

The Federal Trade Commission (FTC) also warns consumers to watch out for fraudulent offers for secured cards. Advertisements for these cards often have a 900 number instead of an 800 number. These calls could cost you between $2 and $50. The FTC also says that any advertisement promising to give you credit is a scam. No one can guarantee credit, and authentic credit card issuers will always check your credit report before giving you credit.

Most companies don't advertise secured cards but do offer them. Check with your bank or search for a secured card at www.bankrate.com.

APPLY FOR A SMALL LOAN

Showing successful payment of a bank loan is another way to add good marks to your credit file. Visit your bank and apply for a small personal loan. But don't spend the money. Deposit the amount the bank lends you in an interest-earning bank account, and use money from this account to repay the loan.

Overall, this strategy will cost you a little money in interest payments, but the positive notations on your credit report will be worth it. Also, if the money you've borrowed is earning some interest, you'll save on the cost of the loan.

Lenders won't know that you've deposited the funds from the loan in a bank account. What they will see is that you're making timely payments.

THE COSIGNING OPTION

Another way to get a loan when you have damaged credit is to use a cosigner. A cosigned loan is one in which there are two borrowers: you and a family member or friend who has a better credit rating. On the basis of the cosigner's good name, the bank may be willing to give you a loan.

If the bank does approve a cosigner, it's a big deal. There are several cautions here. If you default on the loan, your cosigner will be responsible for the money borrowed. If you can't make payments, you'll be risking more than your credit. You'll be risking your cosigner's credit, and your relationship with that person may suffer greatly if you can't keep up with your payments.

But if you are able to keep up with the payments, you'll add some good information to your credit report.

PATIENCE IS THE KEY

If you take some of the steps suggested here to rebuild your credit, terrific. But remember, your credit report won't be shining overnight. Be patient and realistic. It took years to damage your credit, and it will take years to cause large-scale positive change. Every month that you make your payments is a good month, and it will get you closer to a positive credit report.

STEP 8

DON'T GET RIPPED OFF: PART 1

As you repair your credit, you'll find that not all lenders are going to have your best interests at heart. Instead of offering you reasonable credit deals, some may instead try to prey on you. These unsavory types may see that you're in need of cash and that your credit is less than perfect, and they may assume they can take advantage of you.

Of course, not all lenders are con artists or unscrupulous. Most simply want to lend you money, earn a reasonable interest rate, and have their money paid back in a timely fashion.

You need to recognize the difference between a fair deal and an unfair one. And some deals, while fair, are simply too expensive and are probably not worth it.

AUTO FINANCING

Few people can afford to purchase a car for cash. So if you need a loan, car dealerships are more than happy to help you. They advertise low-interest or no-interest financing, and that prospect draws many potential buyers into the showroom. Unfortunately, not all consumers will qualify for the inexpensive financing, and instead, the dealers often have very pricey deals for people who don't have the best credit.

When a car dealer offers you a financing package, there's more to it than just the interest rate. The size of the down payment, the price of the car, the length of the loan, and other factors will all have an impact on what this car may cost you.

Before you even walk into a dealership for a test drive, whether you're looking for a new or a used car, you need to do some research. If you walk into the showroom armed with knowledge, you'll get the best possible deal.

Know What You Can Afford

Before visiting a car dealership, you need to know how much car you can afford. Whether you're looking for a new vehicle or a used one, you have to take a look at your budget to see how much you can afford to pay each month.

It's not smart to test-drive your dream car if you know you can't afford the payments. You certainly don't want to take out a loan if you can't meet your obligations, especially as you rebuild your credit.

If you're still paying down a lot of credit card debt, consider waiting before buying a car. Waiting will give you a few advantages. It will give you more time to pay down your credit cards. Paying them down, in turn, will improve your credit file and give you a better chance at a lower interest rate on a future car loan. It will also allow you time to save as large a down payment as possible for the car. A bigger down payment means you'll have to finance less, so your monthly payment will be smaller and easier on your budget.

Negotiating the Price

Car dealerships are filled with salespeople. Salespeople want to please customers, but they also want to earn their commission and make money for their dealership. Most dealerships negotiate the prices of cars, and that's where they make their profit—the difference between what the dealership paid the manufacturer for the car and what, ultimately, a consumer pays for the car.

When you visit a dealership and look at a car, you'll see a posting on the car listing the options the car has. Each package of options will have a price; and when you add up all the options, you'll have what's called the sticker price of the car. The sticker price is what the dealership would like you to pay, but it's far higher than the price you should be paying.

There's another price you need to know. It's called the invoice price. The invoice price is the price the dealer actually paid the car manufacturer for the car. You should invest in a few guides to buying autos. These publications, found in bookstores and at magazine stands, list the invoice prices. (Or check www.edmunds.com, a free site that gives the same kind of information.) Line by line, you'll be able to see what the dealer actually paid the manufacturer for different options on a car. When you take these numbers and compare them with the sticker price on the car at the dealership, you'll be able to see how much the dealer has marked up prices, and on what items.

When you're ready to negotiate a price for a car, bring your invoice information with you. Question each line on the sticker price, and ask the salesperson to give the invoice price to you instead. Salespeople often say yes on these items (except for really hot-selling cars, for which there's usually a waiting list) because their goal is to sell you a car. They're willing to take a lower profit than what the sticker is asking for.

Dealers can even sell cars at a price lower than the invoice price. Manufacturers give dealers all sorts of discounts, so sometimes the dealer has paid a price that's even lower than the invoice shown in car magazines.

Some of the best deals on new cars can be found at the

end of the year. Starting in the fall, dealers are trying to get rid of cars on their lots to make room for next year's models. Manufacturers sometimes limit how many new models they'll sell to a dealer, unless the dealer can get rid of all the current-year models. Check newspapers for ads, as dealers will often let the public know they're trying to clear their lot, and they'll offer all kinds of incentives— such as price discounts and rebates, special financing deals, and free service for a given period of time—to get people to buy their cars.

Any time of year, you'll almost always get a better deal by purchasing a car the dealer already has on the lot. If the dealer has to special-order your car with certain options packages—or fewer options packages—the dealer will be less flexible with the price. Dealers want to unload cars that are already taking up room on the showroom floor. But keep in mind that the models they have may already be equipped with options you don't need. If that's the case, the price of the car could be a lot higher than the price you were planning to pay.

If you special-order a car, make sure the salesperson doesn't sell you items you don't want or need. (The salesperson may be trying to make back some of the profit that was lost by negotiating a cheaper price on the car itself.) Extras, such as extended warrantees and rustproofing, are one of the biggest areas of profit for new-car dealerships. They're not always essential, and they can add a lot to your price.

Always visit several dealerships and compare prices. When you have, say, prices from three dealers, call the ones with the higher two prices and tell them the price you were offered at the least expensive dealership. Then tell the salespersons you'll consider buying it from them if they can beat the low price. Quite often, at least one of them will.

Explore Your Financing Options

It might seem that you should first find the car you want, and then worry about the financing later. That's not the best strategy. In the heat of the moment at the car dealership, when you're excited about the car, you might be tempted to take whatever financing deal is being offered. While financing at the dealership may be convenient, it isn't the only place you can go to borrow money for a car.

Financing is another area where a car dealership makes a profit. The dealership makes arrangements with lending institutions so it can offer you a loan on the spot. Also, the dealer will check your credit report before making you any offer, and the offer will be based in part on your credit history.

First, you should understand that no matter what kind of financing deal a salesperson offers, it's worthless unless you have it in writing. The salesperson isn't able to guarantee any offers on financing—these deals come from the finance person at the dealership. Next, no matter how often the dealership has offered no-interest or low-interest loans in its ads, it probably won't give you that deal if you don't have solid credit. Those rates are usually reserved for customers who have nearly perfect credit reports.

Whatever interest rate the finance person offers, you should negotiate. The dealership won't usually give you its best deal at the start. Dealers have relationships with several banks, so they can offer different loan options to buyers. Some banks actually allow dealers to make an extra profit on the financing by inflating the interest rate offered to a buyer. For example, if the dealer offers 9 percent, it's very likely that the loan the dealer is getting from the bank costs 7 percent.

When you're talking to dealers about financing, they often ask, "What kind of a monthly payment do you want?" This is a trick question, of sorts, because depending on how the dealers manipulate the numbers, they can give you just about any monthly payment. By changing the interest rate, the down payment, the length of the loan payment period, or your trade-in price, a dealer can change the monthly payment. (For free information on trade-in values, check www.kbb.com, the Kelley Blue Book site.) Though you need to know what you can afford each month, the dealer doesn't need to know that. You need to negotiate the price of the car first, and negotiate the interest rate next. Determining the monthly payment on the basis of those figures should come last.

Other lending institutions may give you a better loan than the car dealership, so you should check these before you go to the dealership. Almost all banks, credit unions, and online lenders give car loans. You should call your bank and other local financial institutions to see what they can offer. Then visit BankRate.com (www.bankrate.com) to see what deals you can find there.

These lenders will review your credit; and if you're approved, they'll give you a credit limit or a limit based on the amount you say you need. Then, they'll issue you a blank check to use for the purchase, but you're not required to use it.

Take this check to the dealer when you negotiate the price of the car. But at first, don't tell the dealer you have it. Dealers are less likely to negotiate a cheap price on the car if they know you're essentially a cash buyer and they won't be able to make any profit on a financing deal with you.

And remember, as the consumer, you have the ability to walk away from any deal before you sign the papers. If you're feeling pressured during any part of the process, walk away. If you're confused or tired, you might make a mistake or agree to terms that aren't in your best interest or aren't the best you could get. Walk away. There's always another deal to be made.

If You Can't Pay

Like a mortgage, a car loan is a secured loan. The lender either holds on to your car's title or holds a lien on your car's title, until the loan is paid in full. (Personal loans taken at a bank are different, but there are still severe consequences to your credit if you don't pay.) If you stop making payments on your car loan, the lender can actually take back, or repossess, your car. And if it does, you're still responsible for the money you owe on the loan, and you'll have some new negative marks on your credit report.

If a new financial challenge comes your way and you see that you won't be able to make your payment on time, you should talk to the lender, just as you would if you had problems with a credit card. Explain what's happening and why your payment will be late. You may even be able to negotiate a different payment plan.

If you're unable to strike a deal, you need to know the repossession laws in your state. Lenders in some states can take back your car once you miss a payment. In other states, they need to wait longer. In some states, the lender must go to court or serve you with written warning that it intends to repossess your car. In other states, a lender can just send a tow truck to pick the car up from your driveway, or even from a closed garage, with no warning at all.

If the lender repossesses your car, it may try to sell the car to get back some of the money you owe. Depending on your state, the lender may have to notify you about the sale so you'd have the opportunity to buy it back—if you can pay off the loan in full. If this happens, you might also be responsible for expenses the lender incurred to take back your car, including attorneys' fees and garaging your car.

A New Scam Every Day

Consumers who own their cars outright need to be on the alert for a new kind of predatory lending—loans on a car's title.

According to the Consumer Federation of America (CFA), a nonprofit association of about 300 pro-consumer groups, so-called car title lenders are charging consumers what amounts to 300 percent annual interest for small cash loans worth a fraction of the car's actual value. These loans are due in full generally 30 days after they're taken out. The CFA survey, conducted in late 2005, looked at title lenders in eleven states and online. It found that almost half of states permit predatory title lending, either through weak authorizing laws or through failure to close loopholes in consumer loans.

On average, these lenders charge a median finance charge of 25 percent per month, which amounts to 300 percent annual interest. Online loans were even more expensive, with rates up to an unbelievable 651 percent. The survey found the lenders usually require consumers to hand over a duplicate set of keys when they take the loan.

Defaulting on these loans can mean repossession in many cases, and borrowers are often still responsible for paying the debt even if the lender sells the car.

The lesson here: don't borrow money on your already-paid-for car.

MORTGAGES AND PREDATORY LENDING

When most people buy a home, they need a loan, called a mortgage, to complete the purchase. Mortgages come in many shapes and sizes; and before you apply for any mortgage, you need to know what's out there. Unfortunately, while many lenders are reputable, others are unethical and predatory. Predatory lending is an illegal activity characterized by a variety of abusive practices, including charging excessive fees. We'll talk more about it later. First, you need to know what products are available and common, so you can recognize which lenders are being honest. (For more information on the home-buying process, see my book *How to Buy a Home*.)

Types of Mortgages

Fixed-rate loans are loans that have the same payment every month. Most fixed-rate loans last for 15, 20, or 30 years.

The advantage of a fixed-rate loan is that you'll always know what your housing payment will be. This is very easy on the budget. And no matter where interest rates are heading, your loan payment each month will stay the same.

But the fixed interest rate can also be a disadvantage. If mortgage rates are moving lower, and you have agreed to a fixed-rate loan, you won't be able to get a lower rate unless you refinance the entire loan. Also, with a fixed-rate loan you're paying a somewhat higher interest rate than you would with an adjustable-rate loan (which we talk about next). That's because the lender is taking a risk by giving you the fixed rate, even if the lender could earn more down the road when interest rates rise.

If you plan to stay in your home for more than five years, experts generally recommend that you choose a fixed-rate loan.

Adjustable-rate loans have lower interest rates at the start of the payback period, but at some point, varying by loan from six months to seven years after payments begin, depending on the loan, the interest rate will adjust. That means your rate could go higher or lower, so your payment will go higher or lower. These rate changes usually take effect every 3, 6, or 12 months, depending on the loan. There's usually a minimum and a maximum interest rate the loan can adjust to.

If you plan to move out of the house before the rate on your loan starts to change, an adjustable-rate loan could save you money.

The advantage of an adjustable-rate loan is that rates are generally lower than with fixed-rate loans. That means a cheaper monthly payment. And if you're lucky over the long term and interest rates move lower, you could have a much cheaper loan than you would have with a fixed-rate one.

Because the monthly payment, at least at the start of an adjustable-rate loan, is smaller, buyers can usually qualify for a bigger mortgage than they can with a fixed-rate loan.

This sounds tempting, but you're taking a gamble with an adjustable-rate loan. It is something of a risk because you never know where interest rates are going to go.

Balloon mortgages are another type of home loan, and these can be very dangerous. They seem attractive at first, as they usually have a low interest rate and low payments at the start of the loan. These low payments usually last for between five and seven years, depending on the loan. Consumers who may not qualify for a fixed-rate or an adjustable-rate loan may qualify for balloon mortgages because of the low payments.

But these can be a financial disaster. After the low payment period ends, borrowers have to make a "balloon" payment equal to the remaining amount of the mortgage. They must get a new mortgage to repay the loan. But if the borrower is unable to get a new mortgage—and people really don't know for certain what their financial situation will be in five or seven years—they will lose the home.

Costs and Fees

Buying a home can be expensive. There are all kinds of fees charged with a mortgage. Some fees are negotiable; some aren't. Here's a look at some of the most common.

• Interest rates: We've already discussed the interest rate, the rate you're charged for the mortgage. Interest rates change daily. When you're shopping for a mortgage, you'll need to keep an eye on how rates are changing. Make sure you know if you're talking about fixed or adjustable rates, as they vary. If you're investigating adjustable-rate loans, make sure you understand when and how high your interest rate could rise. You can negotiate your interest rate; and the better your credit, the better the rate you'll get.

• APR: This is the true interest rate you're paying when you take into account all the costs, including points and closing costs. You can't actually negotiate the APR, but you can negotiate the underlying costs, such as points.

• Points: Points are a fee paid to the lender, usually paid in cash at closing. Each point is worth 1 percent of the mortgage amount. You can pay points to lower your interest rate. There are plenty of no-point loans out there, so you can request no-point mortgages.

• Loan origination and underwriting fees: These are fees charged for preparing the loan. They generally include a credit check, verification of employment, property appraisal, and the time and work spent making the overall determination of the creditworthiness of the buyer. These fees are negotiable.

• Closing costs: These are also called transaction costs or

settlement costs. They are the overall expenses you'll pay to close the loan. Some, such as document preparation fees, are negotiable. Others, such as title insurance, are not.

• Private mortgage insurance: If you don't have a down payment worth 20 percent of the property you're buying, the lender may require you to purchase private mortgage insurance, or PMI. PMI is essentially an insurance policy that protects the lender in case the buyer defaults on the loan. The cost of PMI will be added monthly to your mortgage payment. According to legislation passed in 1999, lenders must automatically terminate your PMI in most cases once you reach 22 percent equity in your home, if your payments are current. You can also request that the lender cancel PMI once you've reached a 20 percent equity position. There are some exceptions for high-risk loans or if your payments aren't current, so make sure to ask your lender.

Signs of Predatory Lending

If a lender wants to charge you extra fees that it can't justify, you could be a victim of predatory lending practices. Here's a look at the most common abuses.

• Excessive fees: Every mortgage will have fees, but how much is too much? If a lender can't explain why certain fees are being charged, there's a good chance that they're not valid. Good loans typically have fees that equal less than 1 percent of the loan's value. Predatory loans commonly involve fees worth 5 percent, or more, of the loan's value.

• Prepayment penalties: Many mortgages carry so-called prepayment penalties. This means that if you pay off the loan early—perhaps because you want to refinance the mortgage to get better terms after your credit rating has improved—you'll face a fee. In other words, these penalties are basically a fee you'll owe if you pay off the loan early.

• Kickbacks to brokers: If you use a mortgage broker to find you a loan, the lender may pay the broker something called a yield to spread premium. This is basically a kickback paid to the broker when the broker is able to sell a buyer a mortgage with an inflated interest rate, or a higher rate than the lender was willing to give the buyer.

• Unnecessary products: Unneeded products, such as insurance, may be sold with the loan to generate extra profit for the lender.

• Mandatory arbitration: Some loans require the buyer to agree to mandatory arbitration. If buyers agree to this, they give up their right to go to court to settle a dispute with the lender about the loan.

• Equity stripping: This is found with home equity loans. The lender offers you a loan based on the equity in your home—not based on your ability to repay (which depends on your income). If you can't make the payments, you're risking your home, and you could lose it if you default.

• Loan flipping: The lender or broker may suggest that you refinance the loan several times, often recommending that you borrow more money. New fees are charged each time you refinance, increasing your debt.

• Bait and switch: When you show up to close on the loan, the paperwork reflects higher fees and a higher interest rate than you originally negotiated. The lender then pressures you to sign the deal anyway.

Government Programs

You may be eligible for more favorable loan terms through government programs, such as loans insured through the Department of Housing and Urban Development (HUD). These programs are available to low- and middle-income families throughout the country. For more information, call 800-466-3487 or visit the HUD Web site at www.hud.gov. (The link is also available on the Esperanza Web site.) You can also find a HUD-approved housing counseling agency in your area at 800-569-4287.

The Federal Housing Administration (FHA) is a division of HUD. This agency secures mortgages, allowing lenders to offer mortgages to buyers who might not have the credit, income, or savings to have qualified for the loan otherwise. The FHA can be reached at 800-CALL-FHA or www.fha.gov.

The Department of Veterans Affairs (VA) has special programs for veterans, active-duty personnel, and their spouses. The VA, which will guarantee mortgages, can be reached at 800-827-1000 or www.va.gov (or get the link at our Web site).

The U.S. Department of Agriculture includes Rural Housing Service (RHS), which has programs for low-income and middle-income people who want to buy a home. Loans offered through these programs can be used to build new homes, buy existing homes, or make home improvements. There is no 800 number, but to find the number for one of the local or state offices go to www.rurdev.usda.gov.

STEP 9

DON'T GET RIPPED OFF: PART 2

When you're feeling a cash crunch, the lure of fast money can be strong. Unscrupulous lenders know this, and they're ready to take advantage of you. They advertise with offers that may seem to save the day—money, and fast. They're not exactly loan sharks, as they won't threaten to break your legs if you don't pay. But the fees these lenders charge are so high that these loans may be just as painful. However, armed with knowledge of how much quick cash can really cost you, you won't fall prey to their tempting deals to borrow your own money.

PAYDAY LOANS

Sometimes payday seems far away, especially when your bills are waiting. Some lenders are happy to tap into your impatience, offering to lend you money on the check you're expecting to receive from your employer. But of course, you'll pay a hefty price.

These loans, generally called payday loans, also go by other names: cash advance loans, check advance loans, deferred deposit check loans. Whatever they're called, they're expensive. These are short-term loans, usually lasting a few weeks or less. Here's how they work.

Generally, the borrower—you—would write a personal check to the financial institution that's going to make the loan. You write the check for the amount you want to borrow, plus the fee it will charge for the loan. The lender will then give you cash in the amount you wrote the check for, but it will keep the fee. Then, it will hold your check until your payday, or whenever you say you will have the money in your bank account. If you don't pay back the loan in the time agreed on, there are more fees for extensions.

The fee here is what's in question. Fees vary, but you can expect a lender to set fees as a percentage of what it is going to lend you, or to have a fee per the amount you borrow, such as $20 for every $100 you borrow.

So what will these loans really cost? The Federal Trade Commission offers this example. Let's say you go to a payday lender, and write a personal check for $115 to borrow $100 for up to 14 days. The lender gives you the $100 and agrees to hold the check until your next payday. The cost of this loan to you is the $15 finance charge, which amounts to a 391 percent APR. Then, depending on the deal, when the 14 days are up you either pay the $115 or extend the loan for another two weeks for another $15. You can even roll it over another 14 days after that. If you roll over the loan three times, the finance charge would climb to $60 to borrow $100. A very expensive loan indeed.

Under the Truth in Lending Act, lenders must disclose, in writing, both the finance charge and the annual percentage rate (APR) of a loan. But even if the lender discloses this information, payday loans are simply a bad idea. Not only are the fees outrageous (would you accept a 391 percent interest rate on a credit card?), but they're also going to get you into financial trouble. If you keep spending money you haven't yet earned, you're going to continue a cycle of debt.

If you need to borrow money, borrow smart. Consider loans with fair terms as offered by reputable banks and other financial institutions. You'd even do better with a cash advance from a credit card, though that's not really recommended.

You should also bank smart. Consider using a credit union for your banking needs. Credit unions are cooperative financial institutions that are owned and controlled by the people who use their services. Customers of credit unions are called members. Credit unions are established by people who have something in common, such as members of a church, alumni of a college, or employees at a company.

Credit unions are not-for-profit organizations; and they exist to provide a source for members to have bank accounts and take out loans at reasonable interest rates. Credit unions offer checking and savings accounts, and most offer loans: mortgages, credit cards, and even payday loans. Their rates are generally better than those you'd get if you walked into any large bank. Many credit unions even offer Internet and phone banking services. So before you take a loan anyplace else, see what a credit union could offer.

REFUND ANTICIPATION LOANS

When you file your taxes, you're probably hoping to get a refund from the Internal Revenue Service (IRS). With bills to pay, you're probably really looking forward to getting that money. But depending on whether you file your taxes by mail or online, it could take several weeks or even two months or so before you receive your refund.

Once again, lenders are willing to give money equal to your tax refund right on the spot—for a fee.

Many tax prepares offer so-called refund anticipation loans, or RALs, which allow you to get your hands on your refund faster than the IRS can send you a check.

The National Consumer Law Center (NCLC, a non-profit organization specializing in consumer issues of low-income people) and Consumer Federation of America (CFA) study the RAL industry. For 2004, they found that approximately 12.38 million American taxpayers spent $1.6 billion to get fast refunds using RALs. (The study by CFA and NCLC is called, "Still a Bad Deal: Beware of Quick Tax Refund Loans." It can be found at www.consumerfed.org.)

The groups say that RALs cost from $29 to $120 in loan fees, and some tax preparers also charge so-called administrative or application fees. And for an extra fee of between $20 and $39, consumers can get same-day loans.

When you take all these fees and compute the annual interest rate for RALs, it can rage from about 40 percent (for a loan of $9,999) to more than 700 percent (for a loan of $200). If administrative fees are charged and included in the calculation, the annual rate of RALs ranges from about 70 percent to more than 1,800 percent.

For this year, the study says, an RAL for the average refund of around $2,150 will cost about $100. A loan under those terms bears an effective APR of about 178 percent. If the taxpayer goes to a preparer who charges an additional $30 administrative fee, the effective APR including the administrative fee would be 235 percent. Add tax preparation fees to the charges and you get a grand total of $276 on average, according to the study. Plus, if the taxpayer wants an "instant" same-day RAL, you can add an extra $20 to $39.

Low- and middle-income taxpayers are the most common users of RALs. According to the Internal Revenue Service (IRS), 79 percent of RAL borrowers in 2003 had adjusted gross income of $35,000 or less.

Critics say that the money used to pay for these loans—

refunds from the Earned Income Tax Credit, which we'll talk about in Step 10—is supposed to help low-income families, but instead is going into the pockets of lenders. They also argue that the true percentage rate is hidden from consumers because extra fees aren't taken into account when lenders explain interest rates to customers. And because of the complicated filing procedure to receive the Earned Income Tax Credit, taxpayers often hire commercial tax preparers who offer these loans. That effectively puts needy consumers right in the hands of questionable lenders.

Instead of turning to an RAL, you can get your money fast on your own, and without large costs and fees. The fastest way to get your refund is to file your return electronically. Most tax preparers offer this service, or you can file your own taxes online. When you file, you can tell the IRS to deposit your refund directly into your bank account. You simply provide your bank account number and the routing number, which is printed on the lower portion of your check. You can expect to receive your refund in about 10 days, without additional charges.

If you're looking for a tax preparer to file on your behalf, find one through Volunteer Income Tax Assistance (VITA), which is sponsored by the IRS. These tax preparers will file your taxes free of charge (for low- and moderate-income taxpayers). To find one, call the IRS help line at 800-TAX-1040 or visit the IRS Web site at www.irs.gov.

COSIGNED DEBT

We've already talked about how you may, under certain circumstances, want to ask someone to cosign a loan for you. But you need to avoid becoming a cosigner yourself, especially once your credit is repaired.

Cosigning a loan means that you're putting your name

on a loan. If the main borrower defaults on the loan, you're going to be responsible for making the payments. And if you can't afford to pay, it's your credit report that's going to be damaged.

Under federal law, the lender is required to give you written notice that explains your commitment to the loan. It will tell you the following.

• If the borrower doesn't pay the debt, you will have to.

• If the borrower doesn't pay, you may be liable for late fees and collection fees in addition to the entire amount the borrower owes.

• Depending on state law, the lender may have the option of trying to collect the debt from you before trying to collect from the main borrower. That could mean lawsuits or garnished wages if you don't pay.

Even if the lender doesn't ask you to pay, the damage to your credit report could mean that you won't be able to get loans that you need for your own purposes. Creditors will see this loan come up as part of your debt obligations.

Cosigning a debt can really be asking for trouble. If, despite this, you decide to go ahead and cosign a loan, there are some steps you can take to gain some protection.

Before you sign, if you do, you can ask the lender to limit your obligations, such as late fees or other costs. The lender may be willing to change the contract to lessen your liability if the main borrower doesn't pay.

Ask the lender to agree to notify you if the main borrower is late or misses a payment. That will give you some time to make back payments before the loan goes into default and real damage is done.

STEP 10

AVOID MAKING THE SAME MISTAKES AGAIN

There's more to your financial life than having good credit. But your credit will be one of the building blocks for reaching your goals in life. Whether you want to own your own home, save for college and retirement, or simply stop living from paycheck to paycheck, you have the power to improve your financial well-being. Once you get your spending under control and start paying your bills on time, you can turn your attention to the future.

MAINTAIN SELF-CONTROL

Throughout this book, we've discussed the steps you can take to gain control over your money habits. No one is perfect, and making an occasional unnecessary purchase or two is to be expected. But you need to remind yourself of your long-term goals. Before you buy something—especially when you're not spending cash—ask yourself if the purchase will further your goals. Are the new clothes or the household items you're buying worth the delay they will mean for your other goals? Every dollar you spend that's not put toward reducing your debt or saving for the future will slow down your progress toward your other goals.

Make sure that you periodically evaluate your credit and spending philosophies. The repayment schedule you set is flexible. Depending on how things are going, you may have to slow down, or you may be able to speed up your plan. Every few months, take another look at your overall plan and see what changes have to be made.

No matter how hard it gets, remember to stick to your budget. This is your main tool for controlling your spending. Taking a look at the end of each month will allow you to tweak your plan. If you spend too much on dining out during one month, you can readjust your plan for the next month. If you allotted more funds than you needed for any goal, you can redirect those dollars to better suit your needs.

Here are some more ideas for finding extra room in your budget.

• Consider working more: Everyone needs time off, but if paying off your debt is your goal, you may want to consider taking on some more work to accelerate your debt payments. One extra shift, or an extra $25 or $50 a week that can go toward debt payments, will make a huge difference in the long run. Perhaps you can work some overtime or choose one night a week for a new part-time job. New work could also mean employee discounts, so consider getting a job in a store where you shop often. Saving 15 percent or more on purchases could be worth more than the actual paycheck you receive.

• Spare change: At the end of the day, many of us empty our pockets or purses, taking out the coins, the spare change from the day's purchases. Get a big jar, and dump your change there. At the end of the month, take the change to the bank and use the money for an extra debt payment. Small coins can add up substantially over time.

• Review your budget: Take another look at your budget. Could your family live without one of those meals out each week? Dinner out for a family of four, unless you're just buying a pizza, will cost you at least $20. That

$20, four weeks a month, will give you $80. You'll use some of that $80 for groceries to cook at home instead, but the rest can go straight to your debt.

• Redirecting payments: When you finish paying a debt, congratulations! Not only have you cleared out some of the money you owe, but you've also freed up some money each month. Take a car payment of $250 per month. Say you've paid off the car. Continue paying that $250 a month, but instead of paying for your car, send it to a credit card. Or put it in a savings account. Put it anywhere but your pocket. This is a perfect opportunity to have a chunk of money—each month—to help you reach your long-term goals.

• Use your raise: If you're lucky enough to get a raise at work, here's more money at your disposal to help you reach your goals. It's tempting to spend the extra cash, but resist. Look again at your budget, and increase what you're paying on one of your debts. Base the increase on the amount of your raise. If you're earning an extra $20 a week, or $80 a month, increase one of your debt payments by that much. And if you've paid your debt, increase your savings by the amount of the raise.

PAY YOURSELF FIRST: SAVINGS PLANS

Pay yourself first. This is something that advocates of savings accounts and investment accounts have been preaching for ages. What does it mean? Paying yourself first means that before you pay your bills, you should set a little money aside for yourself. Not money for a rainy day or to spend on frivolous purchases, but money for a long-term goal.

While your debt is high, paying yourself first isn't the best idea. Though you want to have money in the bank, it's more important for you to reduce your debt. But once your debt burden is under control, "Pay yourself first" should be your mantra.

Getting yourself on a savings plan is easy. The first thing to do is make sure you don't leave your ability to save up to chance. Don't depend on yourself to set money aside in a separate account. The temptation to use these funds is too great. Instead, take advantage of so-called automatic savings plans.

Automatic savings plans are exactly what the name suggests. You tell a financial institution to take money either directly from your paycheck or from your checking account at regular intervals. It then deposits the money on your behalf in a separate account. You can choose the kind of account the funds are saved in, and there are many choices, depending on your plans for the money.

Whatever kind of account you're thinking about, and whatever goal you have in mind, look at these numbers. Saving $25 a month for 10 years will give you $3,000. For 20 years, it will be $6,000—and that doesn't count interest. If these are long-term funds, invested in the stock market (which we'll talk about in a moment), and if the funds earn an average of 8 percent a year, your account will be worth $14,725 in 20 years. Fifty dollars a month in that same scenario would be worth $29,451. Pretty good. Imagine how your money could grow if you set aside more.

Emergency Funds

The first type of savings account you should establish is known as an emergency fund. An emergency fund, as the name implies, is a bank account in which you keep funds for emergencies. This is the extra cash you'd turn to if you ever lost your job, couldn't afford to pay cash for a vital home repair, or had another unexpected expense.

Experts say the general rule of thumb is that your emergency fund should be equal to three to six months' worth of expenses. If you add together all your monthly bills and multiply this sum by three, that's the amount you'd need to have in an emergency fund worth three months of expenses.

That probably sounds like a lot, and, yes, it is. But an emergency fund is the next reasonable step to take if you want to have a backup plan in case you run into money troubles.

How to start? With small, baby steps. Can you find even $10 a month to set aside in a fund that you won't touch, unless there's a financial crisis? You probably can. Start with whatever amount you can live without. Then open an account to be used solely to house these funds. It should be a bank savings account or, even better, a money market account (offered through banks). Money market accounts are essentially savings accounts that pay better interest. And with many financial institutions, the more you have in the account, the larger the amount of interest you'll be paid. Though you might be able to earn more by investing the money in the stock market, the emergency fund isn't money you can afford to lose.

So either resolve to deposit the funds each month, or see if your employer will allow you to deposit funds directly from your paycheck into your emergency fund. If your employer offers this, you'll probably fill out a form telling the employer how much to deposit, and how often, into what account. You'll have to supply the account number and the bank's routing number, which you can get when you open the account. That way, you won't even have to think about setting the money aside. It's on autopilot for you.

Once your emergency fund is set, you can think about

longer-term goals. If you want to start an account for a down payment on a house, for example, use the same strategy. But if you're thinking of a really long-term arrangement—for retirement—it's time to talk about investing.

The Stock Market

The stock market is no place for money you can't afford to lose. But if you're not planning to use the money until 20 or 30 years down the road—as with accounts you may want to set aside for retirement—you need to, and should, take some risk with the money. That means investing.

The stock market is a complex machine, but anyone can understand the basics. Stocks are simply ownership in a company. When you buy a share of stock, you buy a small piece of the company. When the company's business does well, or the outlook for its future is positive, the stock's value will go up. When the company is facing hard times, the stock price may go down. No one—not even the stock market analysts who talk on television—knows where stocks will go and which ones will make money.

But historically, over time, stocks as a group have made money—lots of money. During some years their value may go up; in other years it may go down. But on average, over time, the stock market is the place to build wealth.

By looking at a company's history, its business plan, its products, and its customers, watchers can learn a lot about that company. But let's be realistic—who has the time? The professional money managers do. These are the men and women who make big money decisions for large and small investors alike. If you, like most investors, don't have the time to devote to all the research, you should consider investing in mutual funds.

Mutual funds are simply baskets of stocks. The stock

picker, called a mutual fund manager, looks at the entire stock market and decides which stocks he or she thinks will make money. The fund manager then pools the money from investors—people like you and me—who are interested in investing, and the manager purchases individual stocks that he or she thinks will earn money over the long term. Those stocks go into the basket, the mutual fund.

Mutual funds come in hundreds of flavors. They all have different objectives, and they use different strategies to reach their goals. Some managers buy growth stocks, which are supposed to grow fast; others buy value stocks, which are supposed to be slow and steady. Others concentrate on one area of the stock market, such as health care or technology stocks. Still others are known for conservative investing, or for being more aggressive, or for being moderate—somewhere in the middle.

Which fund is right for you depends on several factors, including your goals, how many years you're planning to keep the money in the account (called your time horizon), and your tolerance for risk. "Risk tolerance" is a measure of how much the ups and downs of the stock market may make you nervous or upset about your account. If you're investing for the long term, you have time to withstand the years when the stock market and your mutual fund will do poorly. There are no guarantees, but overall, over time, you'll probably make money. If you can start investing in a mutual fund through an automatic investment plan, and then forget the money is there, you'll see growth over the long term.

Long-Term Savings Plans

If you're ready to save for retirement, you have several options. The first to consider, if you have one, is your employer's retirement plan.

Depending on the type of company you work for, you may be able to invest in a 401(k) or a 403(b) plan. These names come from the tax code that created the plans. You are allowed to contribute a percentage of your salary to a plan, and then you can choose from among several mutual funds for your contributions to be invested in. In 2006, you're allowed by law to contribute a maximum of $15,000. If you're over age 50, you're allowed to make an extra $5,000 "catch-up" contribution. It's a lot of money, and you're not required to invest that much. You decide how much you can afford to save, and save it.

There are several advantages to employers' plans.

- They're convenient: You tell your employer how much you want to save, and the funds are taken directly out of your paycheck. You don't have to remember to set aside the funds, and you won't be tempted to spend money that's never put into your hands.

- They give tax savings: The funds you save in an employer plan are pretax. That means the money is taken from your paycheck before taxes are taken out. So if you earn $25,000 a year and you decide to invest $3,000 in your employer's plan, the entire $3,000 goes to the account, not $3,000 less whatever you'd owe in income taxes on that amount. Then when you file your tax return, you're being taxed, in this example, on a total income of $22,000, not $25,000, potentially lowering your overall tax liability. Here's another way to look at it. If you invest $20 from your paycheck, you'll see only about $16 less in your check, because the $20 was invested before taxes. That same $20, paid to you after taxes, would be worth about $16.

- The money grows tax-deferred: As the money grows, you don't have to pay taxes on the earnings in the account (as you would if you invested in a mutual fund outside of an employer plan). Here's an example. Say you invest $50 a month in an employer retirement plan, and the fund earns 8 percent a year, on average, over 20 years. The fund would be worth $29,451 in 20 years. If you invested the same amount and earned the same in a mutual fund that was not tax-deferred, your account would be worth only $26,136—because of the taxes you had to pay as time passed. If you can invest tax-deferred, you should.

Because funds saved in an employer plan are earmarked for retirement, you'll face a stiff penalty if you decide to withdraw the money before you're 59½ years old. You'll face a 10 percent penalty and also owe taxes on the funds you withdraw.

If your employer doesn't offer a retirement savings plan, you can still save on your own, in another savings vehicle called an Individual Retirement Account, or IRA. There are two different IRAs available. One is called a Roth IRA, and the other a traditional IRA.

Traditional IRAs are like another basket, and you can choose which investments, such as mutual funds, go inside the basket. Funds invested in a traditional IRA grow tax-deferred, meaning that you're not taxed on the earnings until you take the money out. You can also take a deduction on your tax return, depending on your income level, for the money you've set aside in the traditional IRA.

Roth IRAs are somewhat different. As with the traditional IRA, your savings are growing tax-deferred. One big difference is that you can't deduct your contribution on your tax return. But another difference is that when you take funds out of a Roth IRA, you don't owe any taxes on the earnings. Every penny you take out is yours to keep.

As with employers' retirement plans, you'll face a penalty if you withdraw the money from either type of IRA before you reach age 59½. There are some exceptions if you want to take money from a Roth, such as a disability, large health-care bills, or a first-time home purchase. And you can withdraw the contributions to a Roth—not the earnings—anytime without penalty. But you're supposed to try to keep the funds here long-term so that you have a nest egg for the future.

You're allowed to contribute a maximum of $4,000 to either kind of IRA in 2006. If you're over age 50, you can contribute an additional $1,000. (If for some reason you open both a traditional IRA and a Roth, your total contributions to the two accounts together can't exceed the $4,000 limit each year.)

There's another incentive for you to contribute to an IRA or your employer's plan. It's called the saver's credit. If you earn less than $25,000 a year (or less than $50,000 for married couples) you can receive a dollar-for-dollar credit on your taxes for 50 percent of your contributions up to $2,000. This is another saving worth considering.

If you don't have an employer plan or if for some reason you're not willing to commit your money long-term to an IRA, you can still invest in mutual funds that are not inside any of these tax savings vehicles. You'll be taxed on the earnings your investment makes each year, so the savings won't be as great, but you'll still be setting aside money for your future.

To learn more about how these savings programs work, and about mutual funds and stock market investing in general, check out BankRate.com (www.bankrate.com) and Morningstar.com (www.morningstar.com), a mutual fund rating service.

OTHER TAX ADVANTAGES

There's additional assistance available for you, if you look on your tax return. The federal government and many state governments have tax credits that may help you save on your tax bill. That will eventually put more money in your pocket for bill-paying or savings programs.

Earned Income Tax Credit (EITC)

The Earned Income Tax Credit (EITC), also called the Earned Income Credit (EIC), is a terrific federal program that can help you save money.

The EITC is aimed at those who earn modest wages. If you qualify, the EITC may eliminate or at least lower the taxes you owe. If you aren't obligated to pay any taxes, or if the credit is larger than any taxes you owe, you'll receive a cash payment, or refund, from the Internal Revenue Service (IRS). The reason: the government wants low-income people to have extra cash if they're working for a living.

Fifteen states and the District of Columbia offer similar programs, available for resident workers who qualify for the federal program. Eligibility in the program won't affect your eligibility to receive other benefits, such as food stamps, Medicaid, or subsidized housing. Legal immigrants can also qualify.

To qualify, you or your spouse, or both of you, must work but earn less than a certain amount. For tax year 2005, to qualify, workers with no children must have earned income less than $11,750. If you have one child, you have to have earned less than $31,030. With two or more children, you must have earned less than $35,263. The limits are $2,000 higher for those who are married.

Your individual situation impacts how much EITC you can claim. For tax year 2005, a worker with one child can receive a maximum of $2,662. If you have two or more children, the maximum amount is $4,400. With no kids, you can receive $399. The actual amounts will vary depending on your situation.

For 2006, the numbers are slightly higher. You can qualify for the EITC if you have two or more children and earn less than $36,348; if you have one child and earn less than $32,001; or if you have no kids and earn less than $12,120. If you're married, the income limit is $2,000 higher. The 2006 maximum credits are $4,536 with two or more children; with one child, $2,747; and with no kids, $412.

You can also receive the EITC not as a lump sum after you file your taxes, but as money spread out through the year, coming as part of your paycheck. This is a great way to regulate your budget.

To apply for the credit, you must file a tax return with the IRS and complete the required forms.

Child and Dependent Care Credit

This credit may be available to you if you pay someone to watch your kids (under age 13) or another dependent (such as a spouse or parent who cannot care for himself or herself) while you're at work.

The credit is a percentage, based on your adjusted gross income, of the amount of work-related expenses for child and dependent care you paid to a care provider. The credit can range from 20 to 35 percent of your qualifying expenses, depending on your income. For 2005, the maximum possible credit ranges from $600 to $1,050 for one dependent, and from $1,200 to $2,100 for two or more dependents.

To qualify, you must have earned income from wages, salaries, or tips. If you're married, both you and your spouse must have earned income, unless one was a student or unable to care for himself or herself.

Child Tax Credit

If you have a minor child, you can probably take this tax credit. If your child is a citizen, resident, or national of the United States; is under age 17 at the end of the tax year; and shares your home for more than half of the tax year, you can call your child a dependent.

In general, the Child Tax Credit is limited by your income tax liability. If the credit gives you more money than you would owe in taxes, your tax bill would be reduced to zero, but you won't get cash back. But if the amount of your Child Tax Credit is greater than the amount of your income taxes, and you can claim additional children, you could get some money back. And if you qualify, you can still receive the Child and Dependent Care Credit and the Earned Income Tax Credit.

EPILOGUE

Now we have an understanding and a method to go about developing and enhancing your credit. Yet there are those who may feel that it is too late to rectify their standing. It is important to understand that no matter what your credit situation is, you can in fact change your future. You now have the knowledge you need to make a positive change.

Even those in the most desperate situations have the option of filing for bankruptcy. Hundreds of thousands of Americans have gone through bankruptcy but have normal credit today. Unfortunately there are some who, even after going through bankruptcy, cannot seem to get a handle on living within their means.

Earlier I shared a sacred text that defined the love of money as a source of all kinds of evil. There are in fact many ways that we can develop a spiritual discipline to help us overcome the need and/or desire to spend resources we do not have. Well over half a century ago a world-famous preacher, Norman Vincent Peale, wrote a book entitled *The Power of Positive Thinking*. In it he shared a system that many people of faith have used over thousands of years to battle and combat self-doubt. Many people have "poor credit habits" due to lack of knowledge, but others also suffer from a feeling that they are unable to harness their spending.

The following are ten simple, workable rules for overcoming our inability to control parts of our lives. These rules also work as a method to help us practice our faith. Thousands have used these rules, reporting successful results. Undertake this program, and you, too, will build up confidence in your powers. You, too, will have a new feeling of power and control of your spending.

1. Stamp an indelible picture in your mind of yourself succeeding. Hold this picture tenaciously. Never permit it to fade. Your mind will seek to develop this picture. Never think of yourself as failing; never doubt the reality of the mental image. The mind always tries to complete what it pictures, so always picture success no matter how badly things seem to be going at the moment.

2. Whenever a negative thought concerning your personal powers comes to mind, deliberately voice a positive thought to cancel it out.

3. Do not build up obstacles in your imagination. Depreciate every so-called obstacle. Minimize them. Difficulties must be studied and efficiently dealt with. They must be seen for only what they are and not inflated by fear.

4. Do not be awestruck by other people and try to copy them. Nobody can be you as efficiently as YOU can. Also remember that most people, despite their confident appearance and demeanor, are often as scared and doubtful as you.

5. Repeat these dynamic words ten times a day: "If God be for us, who can be against us?" (Romans 8:31). (Stop reading and repeat them NOW, slowly and confidently.)

6. Get a competent counselor to help you understand why you do what you do. Learn the origin of your feelings of inferiority and self-doubt. Self-knowledge leads to a cure.

7. Ten times each day practice the following affirmation, repeating it out loud if possible: "I can do all things through Christ which strengthens me" (Philippians 4:13). Repeat those words NOW. That magical statement is the

most powerful antidote on earth to inferiority thoughts.
8. Make a true estimate of your own ability, then raise it
10 percent. Do not become egotistical, but develop a whole-
some self-respect. Believe in your own God-released powers.
9. Put yourself in God's hands. To do that, simply state,
"I am in God's hands." Then believe you are NOW receiving all the power you need. Feel it flowing into you. Affirm
that "the kingdom of God is within you" (Luke 17:21) in
the form of adequate power to meet life's demands.
10. Remind yourself that God is with you and nothing
can defeat you. Believe that you now RECEIVE power
from Him.

If we can believe the sacred texts and can apply them to
our lives, we should be able to begin a step-by-step trans-
formation of our credit and spiritual lives. This is neither
a simple prosperity program nor a get-rich scheme. Those
do not work! This is a disciplined approach to saving and
spending that can help you and your children, family, and
friends. As you begin to recognize the power of money as
a tool for investing in your life, you will eventually discov-
er that it can affect every facet of your present and future.
You are now on the cusp of beginning to understand what
God desires from you when your credit is restored. You
will have the opportunity to use your money to effect positive change in your family, friends, neighborhood, community, even in this nation and internationally, just by
where you decide to give something as simple as a $25
donation. When we join our small gifts to the small gifts
of others, we can see how many great things are accom-
plished. All these things will open to you when you take
that first step in improving your credit. Take that step
now. I invite you to go to www.esperanza.us, where you
will find more information on this topic.

ACKNOWLEDGMENTS

I want to thank my family, who had to put up with me while I worked on this project. To my work colleagues, Ms. Larsen and the Reverend Del Valle, thanks for your contributions. A very special thanks to Karin Price Mueller for your tremendous effort on making this book helpful and accessible to our community. I am hopeful that we can work together again in the future. To Reed C. Fraasa, CFP, and Michael Gibney, CFP, of Highland Financial Advisors in Riverdale, New Jersey, thanks for assisting us with fact checking. My sincere appreciation goes to Judith Curr, publisher of Atria Books, for being a visionary and for encouraging this series to go forward. Thanks to my editor, Johanna Castillo, for her great patience and for her willingness to go the extra mile to get this book out to the public. Also to Amy Tannenbaum for her help and support. Thanks to the wonderful Atria Books team: Gary Urda, Michael Selleck, Sue Fleming, Christine Duplessis, and Melissa Quiñones, who have made so many contributions.

SOURCES

American Bankruptcy Institute (www.abiworld.com)
BankRate.com (www.bankrate.com)
College Board (www.collegeboard.org)
CardWeb.com, Inc. (www.cardweb.com)
Consumer Federation of America (CFA)
   (www.consumerfed.org). Survey: "Driven into Debt: CFA
   Car Title Loan Store and Online Survey"
Equifax: 800-685-1111 (www.equifax.com)
Experian: 888-EXPERIAN, 888-397-3742
   (www.experian.com)
Federal Reserve (www.federalreserve.gov)
Federal Trade Commision (www.ftc.gov)
FindLaw.com
Newark Star-Ledger
Mvelops.com (www.mvelopes.com)
National Foundation for Credit Counseling (www.nfcc.org)
TransUnion: 800-916-8800 (www.transunion.com)

ABOUT THE AUTHORS

Reverend Luis Cortés Jr. is the president and CEO of Esperanza USA (www.esperanza.us), the largest Hispanic faith-based community-development corporation in the country. In January 2005, he was featured as one of *Time* magazine's "25 Most Influential Evangelicals." He is a noted speaker throughout the country.

Karin Price Mueller is an award-winning writer and television producer. She is a personal finance columnist for *The Star-Ledger,* New Jersey's largest newspaper; and a frequent contributor to magazines, including *Ladies' Home Journal.* Mueller is the author of *Online Money Management* (Microsoft Press, 2001). She started her career in television, as a producer for CNBC and CNN-fn. She lives in New Jersey with her husband, three kids, one dog, and two leopard geckos.

Printed in the United States
By Bookmasters